Silent A[...]

Five Hu[...]

A Story of Betrayal, Deceit and Murder in World War I

John Dion

© 2024 John Dion. All rights reserved.

Copyrights

No part of this publication may be reproduced, distributed, or transmitted in any form or by any means, including but not limited to photocopying, recording, or other electronic or mechanical methods, without the prior written permission of the publisher. The only exceptions to this restriction are brief quotations used in critical reviews and certain other noncommercial uses that are permitted by copyright law.

For any other form of reproduction or distribution, explicit permission must be sought from the publisher. Requests for such permission should be addressed to John Dion. When making a request, please provide a detailed description of the intended use, including the title and author of the work you wish to reproduce, the format in which it will be published or distributed, the audience it is intended for, and the number of copies you plan to produce or distribute.

Table of Contents

CHAPTER 1 4

CHAPTER 2 25

CHAPTER 3 46

CHAPTER 4 65

CHAPTER 5 71

CHAPTER 6 84

CHAPTER 7 93

CHAPTER 8 112

CHAPTER 9 129

CHAPTER 10 136

CHAPTER 11 150

CHAPTER 12 157

CHAPTER 13 177

CHAPTER 14 189

CHAPTER 15 196

CHAPTER I

It was a warm sunny afternoon in Chicago 1937, we were all playing outside and stopped abruptly when mom told us dad was on his way home, we forgot our chores after school. I was just a kid who did not know much about life at age ten but what I did know is we had expectations to live up to. If chores were not done, mom would have to intervene so he would not lose his temper, she always stuck up for us. He was not a mean person looking to hurt his kids, but he was extremely strict, and we did not want to see that. Fortunately, we were all wrapped up including putting our sports gear away and he was none the wiser that we almost forgot. We lived on a nice block in a modest home and had one car, which he used for work. His salary covered all expenses while mom managed the house and us troublemakers as she would call us. Any shopping mom had to do was within walking distance, and she would use our Radio Flyer red wagon to tote it all around, and of course we went with her for support. He worked as an executive at the William Grant Company, makers of military weapons and supplies, working diligently to stay ahead of the rising costs for a family of four and was adamant about watching current trends of the world. At six foot-seven inches he towered above most people and was not one to back away from trouble, something mom had been trying to fix for years. He had a rough exterior with a strong jaw, he served in World War I from 1916-1918 and was now approaching forty years of age. To enlist he lied about his age as most young men did then, this is his country, and he will fight. In his youth he was six feet, not having sprouted completely yet. His uniform looked like it was ten sizes too big in his photos, he was just one hundred and fifty pounds when he enlisted. He was sent to combat at the Western Front, at sixteen years old he was the youngest in his troop and would end up being a hero. The fighting was ferocious, and soldiers fell by the dozens, every man on the line had to wonder if they were next, I cannot imagine the terror in their minds and hearts. This war started in 1914 and went through 1920, American joined forces against Germany in June of 1917, landing in France. Each day the war turned for the worse, houses being blown up with their families inside, towns destroyed, water and food chain supplies tainted, and hundreds of dead bodies sprawled throughout the communities. Fresh supplies were in demand, clothing, food, water, guns, and ammunition were always running low. The troops ran day and night up hills, across farmlands and scaling walls if needed to get to a safe zone. He had survived battles and lost friends along the way, but he was determined to somehow, someday, come home to his family. On a raw, rainy January evening they were ordered to attack a sector on the South side of Germany, there were eighty-two men in the unit and all eager to defend their blessed country. Upon entering the zone, the streets lit up like lamp posts when the Germans opened fire on them, killing twenty-eight immediately and wounding at least twenty others. Tolson was one of the lucky few at that moment anyway, he escaped gunfire and led the troops to safety to the rear of the broken down, dark buildings. They sit quietly crouched trying to get their bearings in a world they never visited. His body had been beat up in the war and he sported a scar on the left side of his face compliments from a crazed German soldier. His unit was ordered to march through the heart of Germany, taking out all barriers including the enemy soldiers. Nighttime fell fast and the American Soldiers would lie next to dead bodies, animals, and lay in animal feces, better then death at that point. The cold European nights with snow and ice were wearing our men down, they saw an increase with frost bite, pneumonia, bacteria, salmonella, and fatalities. The darkness of night held no candle to the darkness of the war, the enemy eyes and hearts were blacker than that, and the element of surprise was in their favor. The troops were at a disadvantage, and they knew it, the path of least resistance is unknown to them, so they move to flank in the attempt to take out the enemies and make a break for new ground. They split up to cover both the left and right side and charge on command, the enemy now hears us and are on guard, the shooting begins, and the noise is unbearable. Men are dropping at a fast rate for both sides, when the smoke clears, there are but twenty-three of the eighty-two men left in his regimen, a devastating loss. The radio operator pulls out the maps and does his best to define their location and produce an exit plan. They hastily gather as a group when footsteps are upon them, the Germans are not fooled, the United States soldiers are now Prisoners of War. As they were marched toward a concentration camp, they all agreed the only thing they could do was to try and split up and run, but run to where? Two soldiers made the ultimate sacrifice by splitting off and drawing the guards away from the group they were shot in the back like wild animals. The remainder of the unit fought hand to hand with the Germans, they took a brutal beating that brought them near to death, Tolson and five others got away. The Germans are marching violently through the woods to catch them when the Americans open fire and kill all ten in their regiment. There was a sense of calming for just minutes. The soldiers could hear themselves panting and sweat smothered their eyes to a point of blurred vision, they were tired, lost, and hungry again. The dark icy night continued with temperatures dropping near twenty-five degrees, more would surely pass away on this horrible evening. Tolson took control as their commander was now dead and they lost their radio operator, Private Mike Smythe known as "Smitty" stepped up and said he would gladly fill the role. His first command, find out where they are, locate the nearest concentration camp and go on a rescue mission. But they were weak and had not slept in over a full day, they built makeshift sleeping quarters behind rubble and camped for the night. Morning had arrived quicker than they had hoped, with about four hours' sleep they had to find food and water before they could attempt an escape for their fellow soldiers. Nuremberg was discovered to be the next closest town and three miles from there, was one of the largest POW camps at the time, Smitty had done his job, they had a target. As they slithered through the woods and then into destruction, Tolson pointed out a section of town with houses and cafes standing that could have the supplies they needed. Since there were six of them, they broke into three groups of two, they had ten minutes to rummage through the sites and meet back at the base camp they had made. The troop could not afford to lose any more soldiers if they wanted a chance to rescue hundreds of others against a huge German army. They collected what they could, packed it up and met back to have breakfast and draft a rescue attempt, Private Barnes got the biggest pat on the back as he brought back coffee. They built a small fire, brewed coffee, and ate pancakes and an oatmeal-like substance but it was good enough. After finding an area to shower off and changing their socks and underwear, they were ready for the day. Two other privates, Mike Eithel and Tom Higgins volunteered to find more supplies before heading out. Private Tolson urged them to be cautious and look for weapons, ammunition, first aid kits, and any maps they could find. Thirty-five minutes later the two came back with a jackpot, the troops smiled for the first time in days, this was even better than food. Eithel and Higgins came back with sixteen rifles, a slew of handguns and bayonets, and as a bonus, American K-ration foods. K-Ration consisted of three daily meals dry packed in a box, they had collected them from their dead comrades. The troops now had fourteen of these, which would equal forty-two meals. This was ample food for one week, enough to get them through to safety, hopefully! Tolson took time to mull over the last few days events, the death, blood, stench and horrific views of women and children blown up on the streets, how could this be any worse. The private had not seen death like this senseless butchering at any point in his life, now he lived this every day. Their spirits are less than stellar, health is failing all around them, and there was no other radio activity from any U.S. troops. They sat quietly again drinking more coffee and enjoying cigarettes while they pondered his next move. While reviewing maps with Smitty they noticed a hillside that had not been attacked yet, so they set their eyes on getting there, setting up camp, and praying to God that today was a day off from getting shot at. It took two hours to stealthily shift to that hillside where they could plan a rescue, they were able to set up in between huge trees and boulders and stay out of sight. Their minds never stopped working and Tolson knew they were exhausted, time to get sleep. He assigned patrols; three men sleep, three men guard at four-hour intervals, German patrols were light during the day so this would give them reprieve from their attacks. When it was his turn to sleep, he chose to stay awake and review their plan of attack, it must be perfect for them to execute it, all doubts had to be erased from their minds. As nightfall begins the soldiers eat, drink coffee, and fill their water canteens, it will soon be time to move out to the concentration camp. Tolson marches them down the back side of the hills to the outskirts of the town crawling, stooping, and belly sliding, if necessary, their friends needed help. Inside the concentration camp the POWs were starved to the point they were skeletal, beaten daily, and forced into slave labor, there was no glory in that. After walking for five miles, they have reached the fence to the camp, barb wired, and booby trapped along the perimeter make this attempt seems impossible. When it was completely black outside, the group of six headed to the fence to break their way in, they would have to be extremely careful as hitting a mine with a shovel would be fatal. They took turns shoveling as others watched for German soldiers, but nobody had thought about once they were in, where do they look for their friends. There are forty barracks within this camp with upwards of twenty American Soldiers inside each, that is eight hundred people, and they are looking for fifty. Private Tolson's plan consisted of searching barracks one at a time in order, the goal was to connect verbally with an American inside and let them know what is happening. As they go cabin by cabin handing out weapons, they have not seen their immediate troop yet. At last, their soldiers are being discovered and handed weapons, they are scrawny and tired making it difficult to attack full force. The search and rescue team reached the final barracks and found all but twelve of their soldiers, the presumption is they are dead. As they approached the far west corner inside the camp a loud and trembling racket came from the other side, barracks were being blown up with dynamite, the Germans are aware of what is going on. There would be no more time for planning or thinking, it is now time to fight hard and free those they could. A jeep with four German officers suddenly burst through the middle of the camp, Sergeant Denton loaded the rocket launcher and destroyed everyone in and around that jeep, a quick victory that would bring brief joy to the Americans. As he turned to grab his rifle, Denton was shot rapid fire in the head and died instantly, then fifteen soldiers were lined up and executed in front of the remainder of Americans. The Germans were vicious and angry, they threatened Tolson and all the troops around him, either surrender or die where you stand. With nowhere to run or re-group as a unit, the Americans laid down their arms and were beaten, chained, and dragged to a barrack, he was strung up on a post outside to be tortured where everyone could hear him yell. Of the eighty-two American men who marched into battle, only thirteen remained alive and things were going to get worse for them. With blazing fires and piles of dead bodies around, there was no hope in any soul that night, the night was eerier than the one before. The Germans split up the Americans and began interrogating them and physically abusing them, the loud screams of pain rang throughout the camp like church bells in a small town. Additional American troops were headed their way but did not have absolute bearings from their last radio contact, they would now have to track through the same terrain the troops went through. The Germans began whipping and punching Tolson so all the troops could here, his men would weep and feel the agony with him. He refused to give his identification and instructed the others not to give them anything, take the pain and protect our country, do not help the enemy. When the Germans could not break the American soldiers' spirit, they released him from the post and brought him to one of the barracks, he was tossed on the floor like a bag of potatoes, slamming his head hard enough to cause a concussion which would not be discovered until later in life. One of the German Oberst which is comparable to an American Colonel marched in to speak to the POWs. He ordered two of his privates to take Susan's father away to another office and let the soldiers know he was going to be punished severely for acts against them. When they got him to the office, he was offered coffee and cigarettes, a measure to try and calm him so they would get information, he was not stupid and did not comply. They brought in beer and vodka and forced him to drink that while a medic was sticking a needle in his arm, it was morphine and quickly ran through his bloodstream. Now he was tamed, he could feel no pain and was willingly drinking alcohol and gathering his breath. This was destruction waiting to happen, the drugs had slowed his body to a snail's pace, and he could no longer think, he just had to keep his mouth shut and not give away secrets. The drugs infiltrated his internal system further and his body was not feeling anything, and his appetite was gone, the German soldiers went back to the torturing. They smashed four of his fingers one at a time with a hammer, punched him in the face until his nose broke, and then stuck a knife in his thigh so he would have trouble running when the drugs wore off. No medical attention was ever given but they did have a nurse stitch up his leg so he would not bleed to death. The Germans separated all American troops in the camp but were especially damaging to Tolson's troops. They ignored his private strips on his uniform, believing he was the true commander even though he was just a kid. German soldiers left him alone in the otherwise empty barracks, he had a cot to lay on and that is where he would remain until he woke the next morning. His head was heavy and his stomach empty, all the bodily damage done to him under the influence is now radiating throughout him. Every limb, bone, tissue, and his brain were throbbing, and small drops of blood oozed from the less than sterile sutures he received from the so-called nurse. Where was he? how does he get out of there? where were his troops? He soon received his answers when the German officer returned to tell him all his remaining soldiers were dead, but there were still over two hundred Americans here in this camp. The officer had coffee and food brought in and sat him at the table and told him to eat. They would talk after; he was not going to argue after all the torment yesterday. He drank cups of coffee and water, followed by a breakfast of eggs, rolls, and sausages. Although he felt guilty and sad for his men, he would be no help to them if he did not have any strength, he had to do this. When the officer returned, my father was slapped in the face and knocked to the ground again, a nurse pumped him full of morphine and the interrogation began all over. He was pushed for answers to where the troops were, what the next plan of attack was, and who his commanding officer was, Tolson did not utter one word. After four more hours of torment, he was left for dead on the floor of a concentration camp, a dreadful event especially for a now seventeen-year-old boy. The United States troops who were still alive in the camp began to spread out and look for an escape route as they began slaughtering the German soldiers. Hand grenades were thrown in their barracks, bombs planted under jeeps, and German officers being burned to the ground in piles, just like garbage. The Americans have had enough of this torture, it is now time to enact revenge on a country that has burdened others and dragged them into this hell hole. Colonel John S. Kriel of the 41st Battalion took over as the leader, his father was killed in the Revolutionary War, and he had seen his share of lost friends and injuries. He ordered private Dobbs to set up barrack number twelve as the prison for the German POWs, they brought in chairs, desks, and weapons, time for payback. The Americans drilled the Germans with the same questioning, where are your closest troops? where is the next camp? who are your commanding officers? Each soldier refused to answer as expected, they were given the same abuse and two of the officers were shot trying to escape. The Germans knew they were no longer in control of this concentration camp, they were enslaved by American soldiers who planned to rescue their comrades. Colonel Kriel produced a plan to deploy thirty-six men for search and rescue of soldiers and to recon the area within a six-mile radius for vehicles, weapons, food, and new radios. The colonel himself took four men with him to gather maps, medical supplies, stretchers, and any lighting sources such as lanterns, they all had much to do in a brief period. There had been no communication from the Germans to their leaders, so this camp would surely be a target of extinction as soon as they catch on. Six hours after the soldiers deployed, they returned with jeeps, tanks, and the items Colonel had ordered them to look for, they now had a starting point for escape. As the Colonel began his motivational speech Private Henny interrupted and asked if they could raise a glass to the fallen, the private just happened to go into the German Chancellor's office and grabbed two bottles of the world's finest Cognac! A brilliant idea roared the Colonel, let us pray for all we have lost, after a moment of silence the men enjoyed their drinks, warming their souls for even just a minute. Kriel assigned men to lead smaller troops, "you are all leaders now, act like one" he barked, we will not stay here to die, we will move, and the risk is high. The maps were drawn out while radio operators repaired the equipment and began evaluating them for use, all radios were set to channel eight, it was a single lined channel nobody else could access. As the planning progresses, they hear noises outside, Germans they thought, but we have them locked up and nobody has entered the camp, they dim the lanterns and stay quiet. Four soldiers flank the building as they come around the front, there is an American soldier hanging on for dear life, praying the do not mistake him for a German and kill him. As they approach, he holds up his torn sleeve with the American Flag on it, waving it the best he can, he was still overloaded with morphine. He was Private Don Tolson and was now safe for the time being. The privates dragged him in and got him to a cot, there were medics available to start taking care of him, all they could do was try to flush out the drugs and get him to rest. Colonel Kriel ordered guard duty shifts, four hours on, four hours off, he did not want anybody being caught by surprise by the Germans. They needed more time to rest up and be able to move the injured, like Tolson. The men worked hastily to set up stretchers in the back of the jeeps to transport soldiers, a unit was sent out to lay explosives around the perimeter of the concentration camp, when they leave, the last thing they will do is raze the camp and all the German scum in it. A third groups was out on recon or missing Americans, dead or alive they were to be brought back for transport home, families would at least like to have a body to bury. In total, over seventy bodies were recovered, and another fifty lives were saved, it was time to put the plan into action. The dead were loaded into jeeps and covered with blankets, the willing and able helped each other up into the American Liberty trucks, filling both side of the bench seats. Each of the seven trucks had a full arsenal on board including grenades, bayonets, rifles, pistols and bombs, the Americans were about to show ow bad ass they were. Colonel Kriel pulled Tolson aside when he came to, they de-briefed for five hours while the soldiers were getting packed up. Tolson assured him he did not say a word, he provided step by step details of what happened to him and his troops, the Colonel realized this young boy stepped up on his own as a leader. Kriel loved men like this, he wanted all soldiers to be strong in the mind, heart, and soul. As early evening approaches Tolson is better, he is wrapped up, hydrated, and fed, he will ride in the front jeep with the Colonel. As the last truck passes the gate leaving the camp a Sergeant Rollins from San Antonio Texas flips the switch on the detonators, the entire German camp went up in flames, goodbye you dirty bastards, we will find more of you.

CHAPTER 2

The Americans are rolling through the night trying to be as quiet as possible, they were able to access a mountain ridge, and the roads were clear enough to drive fast. It was difficult to keep treating soldiers for their wounds while slamming over bumps and ruts, the medics did the best they could, but more passed away. The four tanks were ordered to ascend the ridge and split east and west, while they moved forward with the deceased soldiers. The colonel used a radio to tell the trucks carrying deceased soldiers to break the plane at the Western front and cross into Belgium and then on to France, the soldiers were to be dropped off so the bodies could be flown home, the men would get their next assignment from there. The remaining trucks were headed south toward Luxembourg and that is where they will cross into France, forty-five miles away. Their ground speed averaged twelve miles per hour, it would take four hours to arrive to see fresh faces, regroup and rest. At precisely eleven thirty at night the trucks arrived at the south border of France and the tanks arrived at the north border of France via Belgium, they were all safe for now. The ride was not an easy one, they stopped often due to German troops marching through the area and had to make repairs. The colonel did not want to open fire, there were not enough Americans to fend off the larger German armies. They were fired upon often and bombs landed in their range, but they managed to take out German soldiers, enough to keep passing through. Colonel Kriel and Private Tolson had much to talk about on their ride, there were answers the colonel wanted but Tolson was reclusive in his actions. The colonel wanted to know why he had taken food from the Germans when you cannot trust them, and why did they fix your leg, they want prisoners and dead Americans, this was not adding up to Kriel. He pulled off the road and told Tolson to get out, they went for a walk where soldiers could not hear their discussion. As they reached the line of trees the colonel punched Tolson in the stomach and kicked him in the leg where he had been stabbed, "give me answers you scumbag, are you a traitor"? The colonel was thirty-three years old, much older, wiser, and tougher; he took no insubordination from anyone, and Tolson was not going to be an exception. At six foot even his voice was like a lion's roar, loud and terrifying, when he spoke everyone knew actions would follow, just as a lion attacks its prey. He grabbed Tolson by the collar crumpling his already dilapidated jacket and told him he wanted an answer, he drew his weapon and pointed it at the private's head, do you want to die here at the hands of a commander? Or do I leave you for the Germans? Tolson began by saying, "you are not going to like this colonel, but I'll start." After the ambush at the south side of Germany when our commanding officer Lieutenant James Morris was gunned down, we scrambled, and I took charge. We escaped the German soldiers as best we could, but they came at us and killed and wounded so many, we lost the leaders. I broke military code and left the men to have sex with a German woman, she lured me into her apartment, and I went willingly. She let me stay after and for three days I lived like a king, the best food, alcohol, sex, and cocaine. I had never even smoked a cigarette before I was shipped out to this God forsaken land of agony, it took to me, and I was hooked on it. The colonel leaned back on a tree and folded his arms across his barrel chest and pondered his next thought-provoking question. Who was this woman? Do you remember her name or where the apartment was? Tolson could not say for sure, but her name was Susan, black hair and about five feet, six inches tall with a heavy German accent and broken English spoken here and there. Kriel told him to get rest, the two of them would leave at three o'clock in the morning to see this area and track down the girl, we need her for more information, she must be a spy, and she reeled you right in dumb ass. Exhausted from the day and the beating Kriel put on him, Tolson passed out immediately, he will need this down time if even for just three hours. At two forty-five in the morning Kriel approached Tolson sleeping in the jeep, he ordered him to wake and make them coffee, we needed to go. Kriel had done research through other soldiers to determine if any of them met this woman, nobody had seen her. He did not tell them why he was asking, he wanted to know if anyone else had played into her hands, they were unaware of her ties with Tolson. Kriel was driving as Tolson's injuries kept him from doing so, when they neared a town that was burnt to the ground they stopped. The destruction was a sad sight to see, bodies everywhere, buildings blown apart, partially standing structures, and vehicles, military and civilian blown to pieces. Tolson sat up in his seat looking panoramically to determine if this was the spot, all the locations look the same right now, total ruins. Kriel pulled the jeep over behind taller structures to stay out of sight, this area appears to have been deemed unlivable and all human life forms had gone, including the German soldiers and their officers. Both men get out and began walking the grounds, Tolson remembers the door had a number five on it and believed the street name was Milne Road, but he could not be positive. Kriel still believes he is hiding something because how would somebody be drugged up, tired, shot, and from another country remember that road, highly unlikely. Tolson showed Kriel how he got away to this side of town and while re-enacting the walk, they came upon half of an apartment building that had the number five on one of the doors. Further down the road was a bent street sign that showed only the letters "Mil," looks like they were in the right spot. Apartment number five was in decent shape given the circumstances, the front door was blown out in half, the windows were gone, but to their surprise the floors were intact, and debris was everywhere. The two men looked at each other and Tolson knew what Kriel wanted, dig through this, and find anything we can on this woman, she is out there, and we need to find her. After two hours of digging through piles, removing furniture, clearing cabinets, and looking at the surrounding rooms they find a clue. Susan had a journal and travel documents that identified her as Leonie, which in German means Lion, a strong-willed fighter afraid of nothing in their lives, she will be tough to track at this time. Even with this current information they have a problem, who can they turn to for help in tracking this woman? Nobody is going to help an American soldier find a German woman. Colonel Kriel tells Tolson to grab a backpack and put the items in there, we will have to move on in the attempt to find help, they jump in the jeep and head back to the base camp they left earlier that morning. Upon arrival at camp the scene was gruesome and eerie, dead bodies everywhere, jeeps burning, soldiers hanging from trees, and a massive bonfire with American weapons, uniforms, and supplied amongst the rubble, a sad sight indeed. "What do you think happened sir," asked Tolson. This is the work of your cocaine addict whore, the reason you screwed your countrymen, just for ass, I should shoot you now! There was nothing they could do as far as removing all the bodies, it was just the two of them, they gathered up all the blankets they could and with what little energy they had, covered up their faces out of respect. The colonel used the bonfire to perk coffee, it had been a horrendous two days and both men have lost comrades they respected, Tolson was diligently trying to make radio contact. There was no German threat to worry about, the soldiers came, slaughtered Americans, and left, no reason to hang around. Kriel poured coffee and they drank it as they tried to erase the animosity between them to solve this problem. Kriel would love nothing more than to see Tolson face a firing squad, he is not worth any more than that to him. The colonel inspected the jeeps as he walked around, if they were not completely burnt out, he would salvage what he could. There was one jeep that puzzled Kriel, it was laying on its side and had two duffle bags that were miraculously not completely burned. He rushed to the bags, dragged them out of the fire, unzipped them, tipped them over and emptied the contents, JACKPOT! He yelled to Tolson for help, they brought all the contents to the camp and began going through them one detail at a time. They sorted paperwork first, there were a dozen documents written in German and code books that could be worth a war if they could de-code them. Amongst the strewed papers Tolson came across identification for the woman he stayed with, birth certificate, license, visa, passport, and a home address, Cedar Rapids Iowa, what?! He shouted out for the colonel to look, he was more stunned than Tolson, the United States? What is this German woman doing with a U.S. status. They dig through and find pictures of her in different disguises, hair colors, and facial marks, such as fake moles, passports, and visas from ten different countries. Kriel's curiosity turned to rage with the more information they found, they had to contact another unit quickly build up resources and recover the wounded and dead. But Kriel wanted the support for military intelligence, Leonie needed to be found, they knew there was something much bigger going on around them, a huge conspiracy within the American troops. At ten o'clock at night, Private Tolson hears noise over the radio, he listens closely for the accent and content making sure he does not jump into a conversation with Germans or American spies. The squelching continues until he hears "this is Alpha five does anyone read me, over," this is Alpha five, copy," we are looking for Americans. Tolson checks his radio, it is still set at channel eight, the voice on the other end is an American, Private Ricky Simpson, a nineteen-year-old from Baltimore Maryland. They converse over locations and Simpson gives them the direct route to their camp, they have scouts everywhere along the German border and are free from trouble. They call out check points so the troops can determine in proximity when they are arriving at the camp. Kriel barks over the radio, "I only want to hear two voices as of now, Private Tolson and Private Simpson, all others avoid radio communications" The coordinates to meet at camp were 49.8941 degrees North and 2.2958 degrees East, Amiens France. Amiens is Northeast of Paris, a quiet community lined with cafes, bookstores, shops and smiles, a change from the last few weeks' events. Tolson arms Simpson verbally with the identifying credentials in the hopes he will be able to track down contacts they can work with to find her before she leaves the country. At four-thirty on the morning of Friday February 9th, 1917, the jeeps carrying Kriel, Tolson and the few soldiers remaining sloshed through mud and slush to get to the camp. They could hardly believe their tired eyes, they arrived at camp with over one-hundred American soldiers, campfires, food, weapons, and supplies. Tolson was taken to medics for a full examination and treatments, he was given vaccines for everything known to man at the time, and he got one for gonorrhea, a gift from Susan. After a hot bath and clean clothes, he felt like a new man, but he was still the same soldier with work to do, first time for food. Kriel gathered the troops and devised a plan to set to catch this psycho, she is trouble for our country, we need her now before more soldiers fall into her trap. A quirky young Private by the name of Scott Dunlap rushed at the group and shouted "hey, hey you gotta' here this," he held out the radio and asked the voice on the other end to repeat. The voice starts their conversation with "this is Major Brendon White, third battalion leader, we are located eight-five miles southwest of your current location, there are two-hundred and twenty-three of us here. We have been ordered to move to you and re-set our orders. Colonel Kriel grabs the radio, introduces himself and asks why they would come back this way, the reply was simple, "we are heading to the Western Front to rejoin our comrades in battle." Major White and Colonel Kriel had a three-minute private conversation, one that shocked the Major but also tore into him like a hot knife through butter. The potential of having a soldier like Tolson who was either completely stupid, a spy, or both, on his team, did not sit easily, he wanted Tolson the second the troops meet up. The radio was handed over to Simpson and Major White's aide simply known as Beast, the information on Susan was presented and the aide went to work with his connections. The anticipation of seeing more troops has brought new life into them all; they are tired, weak, lonely, and morals are nonexistent, relief is a blessing. At two o'clock on the morning on Saturday February 21st, the troops arrive at camp, and they merge as one, there are now over three hundred soldiers in this unit. Major White and Colonel Kriel meet to set up the battle plans, there is no time to waste, we all need to pack up and head to the Germany border, everybody move forward, now! The soldiers rush to pack up and line up the jeeps and troops while the two officers talk about Tolson's problem. Major Whaite already had respect and trust with Kriel, he introduced him to his Colonel Marty

Triana and paired them up to be the 'doers." Triana drops a bomb on them, "sirs, before I came over here, I got confirmation on Susan, her father is an American soldier turned rat bastard to the Germans, we only got this real name, Erwin Schweitz, he is in command of troops on the German border, but we do not know the troop location just yet, from what they did have, he was originally from New Jersey. The officers are enraged, why would anyone turn their back to their Country? Who is this guy and for what exactly did he recruit his daughter? None of the information regarding these two people made sense, the officers sat in brain fog mode trying to figure this out. If they could get to the root cause and reasons, they may save thousands of lives, Americans, Germans, woman, and children. They find no logic in this mystery and need to get on the road, they will review the documents they have and pray for added information as they head back to the Western Front. The troops flank out to three different routes, splitting the tanks, jeeps, trucks, medics and supplies evenly to maintain steady progress to the lines. At the fifteen-mile mark the troops stop for the night; they need enough rest and fresh food to get them to the lines, once there they are back in full battle mode, fighting side by side with comrades. As they near the German border the flashing lights of bombs bursting and the roar of the gunfire defeat any happiness there may have been, "grab your gear and stay low, open fire men, shouted Major White." The troops charged to find the nest of machine gun operators and blew up two of them immediately drowning the fire they were taking on. The battles continued through the days, nights, and weeks ahead, there was no sign of an end, just more dead bodies, and faded hopes of going home. Bullets tear through soldiers' uniforms and grenades take out troops of ten or more at a time, the Americans are ordered to spread out further to enhance their striking power and to remove the substantial number of troops together. In the heat of the battle, Major White still had that girl and her father on his mind and was debating what to do with Tolson. He had no proof he was a traitor nor did Tolson run, so he was not afraid of consequences, but what is the connection? White decided to take Tolson out of the equation and focus on the girl, she is the problem here. He already knew where his private was, and right now he was on the line doing his job and very well at that. Tolson was one of the few who raided the machine gun nest with grenades and gunfire killing over thirty Germans and blowing up tanks and jeeps along the way, he was focused the commitment he made he would not run away from his troops to see a girl ever again. The troops plan is working, they are now surrounding the Germans and taking prisoners, they will use their own concentration camps against them, they will be treated like wild animals. The Americans corralled over one-hundred and ten German soldiers and locked them up in the barracks, no food or water yet. Kriel wants them to think about what it was like for the Americans, there is no way he will treat them like Kings in their palace, the Germans are in for a surprise. They were tied up to posts in the barracks and the barracks locked and guarded, no lights, no fire, no food, or water, sit in the dark and wait for whatever may come. Major White had sent out five recon teams to get intel on that German officer from the United States, they had not returned yet, he had to keep his patience. The troops were disbursed miles apart, there were soldiers' pockets to go through and buildings to be inspected, this will be a lengthy process. The POWs were now being interrogated regarding Susan, aka Leonie, the mysterious English woman who somehow became a German spy, was her father behind this? One or more of these soldiers knew who she was, Kriel was confident with her behavior and ability to lure men in to her world. Days went by without answers until one day a German soldier breaks silence, he wants to get home to his family and will do anything to sell out. He will not talk until he has coffee, food and a bath or at least wash up. Kriel thinks his wishes are minimal due to the information they need, so he obliges him. Private Dunlap hastily summoned Kriel outside. "Sir, German troops were spotted sixty miles out, we have to move fast," Kriel ordered the private to manage this by getting the word to the troops and Major White, we must be on the move in twenty minutes. Kriel asks the German soldier if he likes his meal, he nodded, Kriel offered a cigarette which he graciously accepted. The soldier gives all the reports he has on this girl and tells Kriel where she can be found and what she does for the government. But are his words authentic? If the soldier is lying and gets away, the Americans have another breech point on their hands. Kriel turns, thanks the man for his help and passively puts a .45 Colt slug through his forehead, ending any threat from him. Kriel joins the team at camp, hops in a jeep and moves forward to the battle, more Germans on the way, no time to rest. The American officers meet in a tent to discuss the next steps, they are at odds in which way the attack should play out, but soon that would not matter. The gunfire and bombs were louder and grenades landing ever so close to the big wigs planning the game, seconds later a handful of grenades hit the officers' tents, and they are all dead, Major White, Colonel Kriel, Colonel Marty Trista, and the Major's aide, Private Ricky Simpson. Any information given to Kriel is now gone, the girl does not matter to the troops, staying alive is their only game plan right now. The troops are once again without leadership, who will step up now? A brazen farm boy from Iowa by the name of Carl Riley steps up at six foot four and two-hundred and fifty pounds, he was a force to be reckoned with, nobody disputed his desire to lead. Tolson, Dunlap, and two additional privates raised their hands in leadership; Jeremy Horne from Illinois and Thomas Whiteway from New York. They were each assigned troops of thirty men, given their orders, and sent on their way. Majors Steve Rahway, Marcus Dean, and Gerald Martin oversaw all units along with

Colonels Keith Thomas and Martin Reed. They would give direct orders from their perspective locations, they split themselves up to oversee the troops on the march. Tolson's group led the front while the others flanked and brought up the rear, German troop activity was heavy with gunfire and they had their cannons lines up for field use, the Americans had to act quicker. Colonels Thomas and Reid took twenty troops on the flank and delivered a devastating blow to the Germans. Tanks ran over their jeeps and soldiers, tank portals were opened, and grenades dropped inside killing all. In a matter of fifteen minutes the Americans had destroyed over one hundred German soldiers and officers, they now had control. The Americans' next plan of attack was to move northward along the Western Front and cross over toward Brussels to attack the Imperial German Army twelve miles from there. The Army was expected to have approximately two hundred officers and soldiers, ready for American blood, the attack must be quiet and quick just as this was. The

Belgian Army and French forces were making their way to that area already with hundreds of troops, it was time to send Germany home for good. Four days later the allied Armies all encroached the German camps and executed an onslaught of terror into their souls, over the next five days, the allied would cripple the Germans and send them to their graves. The leaders who stepped up helped the allies rescue the surrounding cities and save their futures, World War I is ending. Thank the Dear Lord!

CHAPTER 3

These soldiers would go on to remain friends for life. They came from diverse backgrounds, towns, countries, ethnic values, and beliefs, but they all wore the same badge of courage; they were alive because of these newly formed bonds in life. The majority will go home and never see or hear from each other again, but those who built strong ties will be friends for life. The Americans are escorted back to France where they will receive their discharge papers and a ride home from the government of The Unites States. Families back home have been monitoring the war via the media, franticly waiting to hear or not hear their child's name on the death list, or blessed to have not received a telegram from the war office stating their son is dead. The soldiers were flown into Hoboken New Jersey from England, the flocks of American citizens smiling and laughing to see these valiant men arrive home. But the laughter does not remain as caskets soon come off the planes and are lined up for identification, families slowly walk the lines with the grim task of finding their child. It was a long week of planes landing, media frenzied, presidential speeches, and soldiers now faced with figuring out what to do with their lives. Othe families had the tougher decision when to bury their sons, daughters, nephews, uncles, cousins, and friends. The early nineteen twenties were full of promise with the war over, streets were full of prospering businesses, stronger economy, and innovation, but the downside was bootlegging alcohol, gang land violence, and corrupt law and government officials running amok. The decade was full of successes early on with Ford Automobiles making up forty percent of the car sales at the time, and unemployment was low, people were working. But in 1929, the stock market crash devastated the country, investors, and businesses, any of them closing. Tolson found a job in a Chicago shipyard as a welder as did veterans who came home after. Three weeks later a guy by the name of Carl

Riley shows up for work, Tolson spotted him immediately, he was in the last barrage of gun battle alongside of him against the Germans. Riley gives him a huge bear hug and they share laughter and sorrow over friends, the union foreman immediately barks at them to get to work or get out, no respect for the soldiers anymore, they were civilians, and the foreman no longer cared what they sacrificed. The two men decided to stop off for a beer after work which turned into six beers each, a long hot sweaty day of welding drives a man's thirst. The conversation starts with the war, friends won and lost, the painful cold, rainy, and snowy days, and even worse nights. Sleeping on cold ground, no protection from elements, sometimes starving, it was survival anyway you found it. Tolson diverted to the sports aspect of life, he loved the Major League Chicago Cubs, and the NHL Black Hawks. He played both sports as a young kid, not good enough to be a professional but he enjoyed it, then came WWI. Riley was a football guy, played tight end for his high school and played baseball at first base, they laughed about how fun it was and for a moment, anything to do with the war was forgotten. They stayed at Micky's Pub until eleven at night, realizing their shift would start again in six hours, it was time to go home and rest. Work was going well but after three months Tolson was not feeling it for the welding world anymore, he was ready to move on, Riley asked him where he was going. He was not sure, he had saved money and was thinking about moving to Michigan to work at the Ford plant, jobs were plentiful there as well with slightly better working conditions, minus the five-day, eight-hour work week created by Mr. Ford himself. One of the local policemen had a nephew who was a manager and was able to get him a job. He had Riley's information and assured him he would contact him with his new address and number when he got settled. Two weeks later Tolson was ready to go, he let the foreman know, shook hands, and said his goodbyes. The next morning, he awoke to a sunny, warm

June day in 1921 and rushed to the table for breakfast, he was hungry, and mom was more than happy to do so for all her children. He packed his suitcase beforehand and washed up a bit. He chowed his food as if he had not eaten in weeks and drank three cups of coffee, something he learned to love in the army. He cleaned up again and said goodbye to mom and his siblings, grabbed his cigarettes and case and he was gone, a new chapter in his life. Barry Tolson was a good catholic boy, he had his share of trouble with the police as a young boy, small time stuff like breaking and entering, stealing a car, breaking windows on a neighbor's house. The police knew the young Mr. Tolson very well, his father was not around much and left them no fatherly discipline or financial support in the house. Barry was a good son; he will continue to send mom money for the house once he is settled. He walked the one-mile trek to the train depot, bought his ticket and bought an ice-cold Coca-Cola to sip while waiting to board, it was getting hotter, his train scheduled to leave at

9:02 A.M. The train pulled in about 8:54 A.M., time to get boarded, Tolson ran to get a good window seat. As he pushed down the aisle he bumped into a familiar face, Private Whiteway from New York. A quick handshake and a hug led to Tolson asking him where he is headed, I am going to Colorado to work on a farm, my wife's father needs help, and we are going to live there as well. Within a minute this beautiful blond-haired woman strolls up to Whiteway and plants a big kiss on his cheek, "who is this young man" she said. There was a brief introduction, and they parted ways, his wife was pregnant and not feeling well so they had to get their seats. Tolson sat thinking to himself how fast life changes, they were out of the war and there is a guy now married and having a baby, he did not even have a steady girl at the time. The path to Michigan was going to be a brutal five hours, he was not a man to sit still for long, but had no choice, he had to get to work on Monday. He had much to think about on the way, where was he going to live? A boarding room for three weeks anyway, where he would buy food, fitting into a new neighborhood and job is not an easy undertaking. Tolson had over three hundred dollars so he would have to get to a bank in the afternoon to not leave all the cash around, he worked hard and saved every dime. The train pulled into the station at 2:08 P.M., just six minutes later than anticipated. It was overcast in Michigan but still just as steamy, ninety-three degrees with humidity. Clothes stuck to everyone's bodies and the sweat dripped down their faces like a waterfall, Tolson trotted back to see Mr. Whiteway and his wife to wish them good luck. Whiteway gave Tolson his address, phone number, and an invitation if he is ever in Colorado, they shook hands again and left it at that. Barry strolls down the main street looking for the nicest yet inexpensive inn for three or four weeks, he comes upon Mary Bess's Hometown Inn. Mary was the busiest inn for miles, she had eighteen rooms available with a bath on each of the three floors and a full dining room for guests. It was a modest home but meticulously clean and groomed inside and out, the food was prepared by local grandmothers and the beds were modern with new mattresses. Her nieces and nephews worked as maids, cleaners, and servants for their guests, Tolson was rented room five on the first floor, close to the bath. He paid for the week up front with cash and grabbed his receipt along with his belongings and headed to the room. As he neared the room he stopped at the door and put the key in the lock, he stood almost frozen in time for a minute, room five! Susan's room in Germany. With an eeriness and chills running through his body, he turned the key and slowly entered the room as if to make sure nobody was there, with the room clear he put his things down and headed to the bath. It seemed like an eternity being in the bath, but it was merely twenty minutes, he had dirt and dust to get off his clothes and had to get those cleaned as well. Once in his room he put all his belongings away and headed to the bank with his money, this was his priority. After the bank he decided to eat at the local bar instead of the inn that night, he walked dup, grabbed the best seat, and ordered a beer and whiskey, this would help me sleep he thought. He phoned mom and his siblings after dinner and let them know he was okay and where he was staying, gave them his love, and went to sleep. It was Friday and he was not reporting to work until Monday, he had time to go through his list of things to do and be ready. He checked off the bank, housing, and laundry from his list, tomorrow he would spend the day walking the town and visiting the worksite at Ford Motor Company. Saturday morning arrived sooner than Barry liked, he was hoping to stay in bed with no chores to do but he was up at six o'clock. He got dressed, went to the dining area, and drank coffee while reading the local newspaper. Mary came in to say hello and asked if he would like to eat now, surely, I would madam he replied so she made him a huge farmer's breakfast with eggs, bread, ham, pork, and bacon! Great start to a day and he could use the weight. After filling his gut, he excused himself from the table and asked if he could take the paper with him. It is yours, she said, have a wonderful day. Mary was only in her thirties and attractive, her husband had died two years earlier in the war in Germany and Tolson had to wonder if he ever met him. He asked Mary what his name was, she replied to him, Lieutenant James Morris. His throat swelled up and he replied, Mary I served under your husband, he was a good man and did his best to protect us, I am sorry for your loss. Small tear drops streamed from her eyes, but she kept her composure as she directed him toward the Ford plant, it was not a long walk and went back to her business. As he walked through town he smiled and said hello to everyone, he was personable, and he will be in town so might as well make friends where he can. He arrived at Ford's River Rouge plant which had just opened in 1917, it was clean, organized, and secure. He could not get through the fence to walk the lot but at least he knew right where to go Monday morning, it was a mere fifteen-minute jaunt. He stopped in the area for a quick lunch at Sammy's Shack, a burger and fry joint with the best chocolate malted frappes in the region, he was a chocolate snob, so it had to be the best. He stopped at the pier of a local park and grabbed a bench seat; he had picked up the afternoon edition of the paper and decided to read it. The sun was warm, the blue sky soothing, and the ships' brows breaking the waves sent a peaceful sound to his mind, a beautiful place to spend the afternoon. As he flipped through the pages and read the local articles, he could not bypass the comic pages, he loved to laugh, this was an easy outlet. Buck Rogers, Popeye, and Tarzan were the big hits and popular with veterans, he smiled and laughed his way through them. He put the paper down for a moment and stared into space, it was quiet and still all around him, this is the inner peace he was looking for. Although he had been home for two years the war was not far behind him, he wondered how the allies and his American friends were doing, and internally mourned those who died saving his ass. He wondered what Colonel Kriel knew about Susan before he died, did he track her? and what of her father Erwin Schweitz? Where is he? Dead? Was he really an American from New Jersey, or a German officer who sired this woman? With all the time he will have in his hands, Tolson needs a hobby, but sports or arts are not in his mind, he is going to find that crazy Susan. She and her alleged father had over five-hundred American officers and soldiers slayed, she must pay the ultimate price for her betrayal. He admired Colonel Kriel even though he kicked Tolson's ass, but he knew he deserved it, he abandoned his men at the time of war, he was a coward at that time. Kriel taught him to be tough and to dig until you get the answers, do not let things go. Private Barry Tolson was now going to become an investigator, he will figure this mess out as long as it takes, his military recon and scouting training will lead him to the correct path. He thinks of how close they all were to getting home alive and pictures of the big attack on the Western Front pop into his head. All the Majors and Colonels taken out with one fell swoop, all dead, pay back is coming bitch. With no writing utensils he packs up his trash and leaves the pier, he is heading back to the inn to draft his plan of attack to solve this disastrous hidden assault on Americans. It was still a beautiful warm evening in Michigan, so Tolson took his pencils and paper and began jotting down what he already knew. He asked Mary to use a picnic table, and she obliged, even offered to bring him food and drink. Lemonade and a ham sandwich would be appreciated, Mary said Tolson, and a piece of that great cherry pie I smelled in the kitchen, they laughed and off she went. Mary was a proud, industrious woman, even before her husband left for the war, she was a driving factor in the success of this inn. Her husband and brothers built it from the ground up with their bare hands and their own tools, but it was solid. Mary and Lieutenant Morris had purchased the land with a small barn on it for just three hundred dollars in

1914 and put all their blood and sweat into the property. First, they expanded the barn to a full one-story house with three bedrooms and an open kitchen to the living area, the land was tilled, and they became successful farmers for vegetables and fruits. In 1917 they had saved a small fortune and with that money added on two more stories with baths and they were on their way to running another successful business. It was the talk of the town and surrounding states that this is the place to stay, travelers could choose to make dinner reservations there and a bath would cost an additional fifteen cents. The Lieutenant had the brilliant idea of adding a barber shop inside so that people could get all their grooming needs addressed while in town or during their stay. Although Mary was a little older than Tolson, she had a twinkle in her eye for him, he reminded her of her late husband; he was caring, hardworking, smart, and charming. The Private began draining all his knowledge onto paper, it was tedious, painful, and sometimes sad but he was making progress. It was hard not to think of the days he spent with Susan before he knew about the real Leonie. She was hot, sexy, and even sweet and she could cook. Her dark side is what he did not miss, the drugs, alcohol, treason, and betrayal of our great country. He wrote down the address where he was with her, the one Kriel helped him re-discover in the rubble, and all the other details he had that were factual, he still had her identifications in his duffle bag, he will look at those in his room when nobody is around. He knows this will be a huge breakthrough when it is over, but this is not a one-week investigation. He was going to have to rely on his old war friends including allied soldiers if he could reach them, this was a big puzzle, and he had no pieces to start with yet. His goal was to keep this private, especially from Mary for now, he is convinced her husband was one of the five hundred, she would be devastated to know he was murdered not killed in war. Eventually, she would find out, but later was better in his eyes. He outlined all the starting points, locations, names, documents, dates, and cities and when he was done it was time to sleep, he had much to do the next day. Tolson started his day out at the picnic table with breakfast and coffee served by his favorite host, Mary. She was curious as to all the documents and paperwork and he politely told her it was a project he was working on so he could get a better job in life, she bought it, smiled, and went in to retrieve more coffee. His first point of attack was to find out about Erwin Schweitz, Susan's alleged father, the most critical piece he got from Kriel before he was gunned down in cold blood. He went to the telegraph office and asked them to send a message to three people: Private Dunlap, Whiteway, and Major Gerald Martin. The letter was addressed in code to state this; "Dear sirs, I am in search of Susan aka Leonie, the woman Colonel Kriel was tracking down with me, he had more information, but I have gathered new data. I am asking for your assistance so we can bring her to justice, please wire back any information you may have. One of you might find clues in duffle bags or letters that were collected at the last camp site before the tragedy, please reply. Sincerely Private Barry L. Tolson" Tolson stood close by the messenger to assure he did not try to read into the code, he told Tolson he would have someone chase him down when he got responses. In the meantime, he went to work on Susan's documents, but he would need a smarter person familiar with document identification and tracking. He went to a local drug store and picked up the phone to call Riley in Colorado, he did offer help if needed. Riley had collaborated with soldiers in the communications office and Tolson needed just one contact. Afte small talk Tolson found out that Riley was the new father of a beautiful baby girl, Jessica, six pounds, five ounces and thirteen inches long, his wife and everybody is healthy. Tolson explained part of the process but could not give Riley everything yet, he promised to fill him in once he talked to the communications officers. Riley gave him Sergeant Kent Jordan and Private Michael

Brock two of the most honorable men he ever encountered, they would help for sure, Tolson said he would call again in about three weeks with updates. As he made his way outside a young boy ran up and told him the telegraph office had received this, a reply from Major Gerald Martin, Tolson gave the boy five cents, and he was on his way. He laid the telegraph on his table with the other documents and opened it up, a Major replying that quickly? He must know something! The telegraph stated, "Private Tolson, you need to arrive at Renaissance Station in Troy Michigan, see the clerk, his name is Tony and ask for the key to box number thirty-three, code word is hen house." He rushed into the inn and asked Mary if he could borrow their pickup truck, he had to get Troy within the hour. It would take about forty minutes to get there, and it had to be today, he starts work tomorrow morning and cannot be late. Mary obliged, she trusted him and had no questions she just asked him to be careful and fill it up with petrol when he got back. He gave her a hug and a huge kiss on her cheek and shouted Thank You with joy! He grabbed the telegram, hopped in the truck, and blasted off to Troy. Upon arrival he asked for Tony, when he approached the clerk, he stated he was looking for the key for number thirty-three in the "hen house," he was graciously handed the key, grabbed the documents, and ran to the truck. He got back on the road then filled up at Pete's Standard Oil station just a block from the inn, keeping the local money in town he thought.

CHAPTER 4

He had no time for sleep deprivation tonight, six o'clock in the morning would be here soon, he sat and wondered about his approach. He could stay awake for another two hours and still get up on time, so he opened the documents from the box and was amazingly surprised, he had given him Susan's last name and her father's real American name, not his alias. Holy lord, what is going on this is such a storm that keeps getting deeper. He read the names aloud to himself, Susan was Susan Gordon, and her father was Brian Gordon, both from Patterson New Jersey, Ten Commerce Road to be exact. He now had a great starting point he thought, something to give to the communications officers for further intel. It is late now, and he will retire and start anew tomorrow. Sergeant Kent Jordan and Private Michael Brock were still enlisted in the Army so that made it easier to get a message to them. Tolson was due at work at 7:30 AM and the telegraph office opened at 7 AM, so he had time. He fired off his message to both men and advised the clerk he will check in after work for any received messages from these two parties. He arrived for work eager to get started as it was something new for him, assembling automobiles, good wages, and opportunities for new friends if he chose. Tolson was proud to be working on a line that built Medic vehicles for the war to carry the wounded and dead, he learned manufacturing on his first day and was not distracted by others talking while they worked. When the whistle blew signaling the day was over, he ran as fast as he could to the telegraph office and saw the clerk, any news yet? Any news yet? The clerk handed him the message he was hoping for, more information regarding the murderer and scumbag father, if he is still alive, I will kill him too, the whole family. This is not how Tolson usually thought, but he was angry now and still guilty that he had left with her in the first place, but this is justice he thought, although it was really revenge. These people were not going to be pulled in for a Court Marshal or sentencing, he would rather hunt them down and shot them in cold blood, he was okay with this. The message contained information of where he may find her and the biggest shock, the German officer killed by Kriel may have been telling the truth but that did not matter anymore, this was Tolson's mission now. He asked the clerk to send back a most gracious Thank You to the soldiers and left for his room, he had time to work after dinner. He checked in with the desk to make sure there was room for him at the table, Mary said 'always young man," everything will be ready at six o'clock exactly, so you better wash up. There were fourteen diners seated for this delicious ham, roast potatoes, and fresh garden vegetable dinner, with homemade rolls, Tolson was hoping for a quiet meal that he could throw down fast and go back to his room. He would not get that with this group, they were all cackling like a room full of hens and the noise was unbearable, but he played along as Mary was so nice to him. A woman turned to him and asked where he was from and why he was so quiet all the time, he looked at her softly and stated, "I just always have a lot on my mind and started a new job." That was not good enough, she was a nosy bird, and the others were glad to chirp in. He opened a bit by telling them he is from Illinois just outside Chicago and he served in WWI and now works at Ford as an assembler. Tolson added tidbits about family and that was enough, he shut it down and turned the tables by asking the other questions. The conversation opened and went on for an hour, he excused himself stating he had to retire for the evening, he was exhausted. He arose early the next morning grabbed coffee and a sandwich, and packed lunch by Mary. She made him a ham sandwich with snacks, and he was out the door. He could not help thinking about Mary on the way to work or while at work, she was sweet, caring, and loving and always smiling, they took to each other. His focus was to catch Susan, nothing else mattered to him, he was driven inside to make this happen and a relationship was not in the cards right now. Each day after work he ran home to piece together the puzzle, he would work on it for hours, have dinner then work again, he repeated this every day. He started eating at the picnic table outdoors so he could concentrate, guests thought he was rude because he did not reveal his activities, none of their business he thought, what do they know. The pieces were coming together but he knew the next problem would be to find her and catch her, this meant going to Franklin Pennsylvania the information that was provided by the communications officers. The trip would take at least four hours each way by travelling for a weekend, but it is the only way and time he could do it. He would plan to leave Friday after work, but he had to see if Mary would let him have the truck for that long, they did not use it often, but it was part of the business. Thursday afternoon he picked up flowers for Mary on the way back from work and handed them to her by the kitchen when he got in, "flowers brighten up a place you know" he said laughing, she said "they sure do." Tolson asked Mary to sit down, and he had a favor to ask. When he mentioned the truck, she did not seem to be concerned where everything the need is within town, but she was getting curious and wanted to know why Pennsylvania. He said he did not want to go into details, he is trying to figure out something from the past that he needs to know, there are people looking for closure. Mary told him she had faith in him and to be careful. She expected to see him and the truck back by eight o'clock Sunday night, he agreed and said when he figures this out, he will let her know. Mary was wise and she understood this must be an internal demon he was trying to alleviate but she would not push anymore, one thing stuck in her head. The fact that Tolson served under her husband, and he was emotionally talking about it, led her to believe this is a military issue. Oddly enough, she always thought something was amiss about her husband's death, wives and mothers always know.

CHAPTER 5

Barry Tolson was set to leave at six o'clock Friday night, he had lots to do after work and had no time to waste. He packed much of his gear Thursday night before going to sleep and asked Mary if she could please put together a road dinner and snacks for him, she again obliged. It was a long day at work Friday, the plant was hot, parts were missing, and they experienced quality issues that day with paint. It was frustrating to say the least but all he could think about was getting on the road to Pennsylvania, he had to put this behind him. At last, the whistle sounds, and everyone says goodbye for the weekend, Tolson jogged back to the inn to get ready for his departure. When he arrived, it was three o'clock on another hot afternoon, so he went to the lake to go swimming, relax, and cool down after a grueling day. He checked in with Mary when he got back, and dinner was set for five o'clock so he could get on the road earlier, he was grateful and stuffed his face! She also packed goodies for the road and asked for a call when he arrived at his destination. He used the hall telephone to call home and speak to mom and his siblings, he had just wired her fifty dollars for food and rent and that would be enough until next week. He gave her an update on his job and living situation and told her he was healthy and doing well, they exchanged I Love You's and hung up. He rushed back to Mary to get the truck keys and ran out the door like a wild bull, good thing he was young and fit, or he would never get around to getting this done. At six o'clock he gets in the Ford Model TT with a 201 CID engine (3.3L), one ton capacity, and four speed manual transmission and heads out. The power load maxed out at 15-17 MPH and bounces down the roads toward Pennsylvania, a journey that will require patience. The trip will take sixteen hours to drive leaving minimal time for investigations while in Franklin, Tolson had a thought, so he stopped off at the next phone booth to place a call to Thomas Whiteway. He once told Tolson he had friends in Pennsylvania and the towns are close to Franklin, hopefully he could get help investigating. Whiteway apologized for not replying to his telegraph, but his parents just died in a fire, a tragic loss. Tolson was beside himself he could not even believe what he just heard, he offered heartfelt, solemn love and understanding to the younger ex-soldier. Whiteway asked him what was going on, why are all these calls and telegraphs you up to? Tolson gave him a quick lowdown and Whiteway wanted in, where can I meet you? I want to help! Tolson asked how long it would take him to get to the Franklin area from New York, "only two hours sir, I'll leave now" Ok Tolson agreed, it will take me twelve more hours, get a pad of paper and pencils and I will call you back at this number in ten minutes, do not screw this up." Whiteway gladly bolted to the local store, he was saddened by his parents and had no siblings, this kept him occupied helping an old ally friend. When Tolson called back, Whiteway was ready for the information, he let Tolson know he was eager and committed. The first information Tolson gave him first was to check out a house with a big farm at 237 Cronan Road in Franklin, all he had to do is search the exterior and see who lives there. Tolson wanted vehicle license plates, steal mail if there is any in the box, and descriptions of the people there if anyone is on site, as they hang up Tolson reminds him to be armed with a weapon, there could be trouble. Tolson picks up coffee and heads down the road, Whiteway begins packing his bag including two handguns, a .357 magnum and a .45 automatic with ammunition. It would be a quicker, simpler ride if he took the train, so he ran to the depot, bags in hand, and bought a ticket. He arrived in Franklin at 8:40 PM and decided to get a room first, not knowing how long he would be here after Tolson arrived. He unpacked, put his .45 in his waistline under his shirt and quietly left his room so he could go to the house without question. His room was only a ten-minute walk to the house, so there was no need to get a ride, he could not have witnesses anyway he thought. He remembered Tolson telling him that Susan is five foot, six inches tall, one-hundred and twenty pounds, ageing lines, about thirty years old. with black or blond hair, he will have to go by that description and her face is elongated with dark eyes, either brown or black. Whiteway entered onto the property a little after ten o'clock with the hopes everyone was sound asleep, they were. First, he documented the two vehicles in the driveway, a NJ Plate number 68572 attached to a 1919 Ford Model T and 287-108 PA attached to a 1919 Rolls Royce Springfield Ghost. His next move was to recon the perimeter of the house to see if anyone was still up, he noticed there was no fire in the fireplace and no lights or lamps on, I am all good to go. Whiteway gently slipped the lock open on the side door as there was a bedroom by the front door, he was sweating profusely at the thought of the man of the house waking up, he was trying to stay calm. With a small light he began poking around for documents as Tolson directed, anything with names, identification, age, addresses, all important. He made his way to the den and began searching in the beautiful antique roll top desk, there was not much there. He noticed on the kitchen table there were papers, and two empty glasses left over from a night cap of moonshine, he grabbed them without reading and stuffed them in his bag, better to get the hell out of the house now. He was curious to see who was here, he got up the nerve and opened one of the bedroom doors, a man and his wife were asleep, he closed that and went down the hall. The next stop had two children sleeping, they looked to be about teenage years and again he moved on. In the darkest part of the house was a door slightly ajar, he thought Susan, this could be the room. As he pushes open further, he is hit with the butt of a shotgun, he could make out it was a female and she jumped out the window, it had to be her, why would she run. Somebody tipped her off, he wrote down the notes and what she was wearing, a white shirt with farmer jeans and work boots, long hair but could not see the face. He had to find her, as he ran, he thought why she did not alert the rest of the house, this is getting stranger, but Tolson would be happy with my findings. He moved stealthily around the house to the barn; no vehicles had been started and still there were no lights on anywhere on the property, she had to be in the barn. Tolson was plugging along to Pennsylvanis, he had a good eight hours left, he hoped that Whiteway was getting information they need and that he does not get arrested, can I trust this kid? Back at the farm Whiteway was circling the barn but she could be hiding anywhere, he entered the doors looking up in case she was in the loft. He moved throughout the stalls and checked behind all saddles stand and climbs to the loft, nobody, not a peep from any critter and no sign of the woman. As he exits the barn, he sees lights come on and a roar of "who the hell is on my property, I will shoot you where you stand." He woke the sleeping giant, this man was huge and angry and came stopping in his direction, where could he hide. He thought back to his training where the flanked the armies out, so he used this tactic to come up behind the big man and render him unconscious by hitting him with the butt of the magnum. He grabbed rope from the barn, tied him up and gagged him, he would still be until someone woke up and found him, he had time. He searched the man's car, found his registration, and packed it in his bag, took one more run around the property and found nothing, Back to his room he fled to sort out the new documents and try to decide where this woman may have gone. Tolson was only about four hours away now and could not wait the anticipation was driving him crazy. The time was approaching 4 AM, he was tired and pulled over to find coffee, the bright lights ahead showed a sign that stated, "Open 24 Hours" and immediately pulled into the lot and parked. Once inside he grabbed a stool at the counter and ordered coffee. He brought in documents to pore over and determine if there was anything he missed, it all looked blurry to him at this point. The diner décor was red and white checkered tables, red stools with a gray counter, only two people were on duty, the server, and the chef, it was not a busy morning. He asked the server how far it was to Franklin, she replied by telling him he was closer than he thought, it was two and one-quarter hours away, not four. He devoured breakfast and coffee and wondered how he would find Whiteway when he got there. It could be small, he thought only two hotels which would not take him long to find. He paid up, went to the truck, got fuel, and off he went to meet up with the other ex-private. Whiteway was in his room reading the new documents, he came upon a major shock, the registration for the car at the barn belonged to none other than Brian Gordon, Susan's alleged father. He had the Rolls Royce with Pennsylvania plates, the assumption was the other car is Susan's, he had to go back and grab the registration before Tolson got there. He compiled all the information he had and hid it in the floorboards under a carpet, he was now going back to the house, a dangerous quest with people on site, the giant was awake by now. This time he snuck around the barn and came on the back; it was easy to pull the registration out and get out safely. As he leaves to go back, he notices a ripped shirt on a fence, he takes it with him, he also notices a woman inside the house with just a bra talking to the big man, this must be her, she is back. Tolson arrives in town and finds Whiteway was walking down the street when Tolson caught his eye, his truck was dirty and dusty as he was, they shook hands and headed back to Whiteway's room. Tolson grabbed a towel and went to the tub room, there he would bathe, scrub his teeth, and get dressed back in the room. Once he was settled, they planned the strategy for their investigation, Tolson was impressed with Whiteway's work, he had accomplished much in a brief period. The end goal was to capture Susan and take out her father, he was a scumbag who sold out his country to the dirty Germans, he deserves to die, painfully if possible. They would have to stay out of sight until it was dark again, but they needed food and went to the dining area at the inn downstairs. They ate with their heads low and did not make eye contact with people, they knew the Gordons would not come into town, but they wanted no messages getting back to him that they were in town. He would put two and two together and know it was them coming after him. They went back to the room to sleep and would leave at 7 PM for the house and do their best to get Susan. Tolson awoke first and gave his partner in crime a push to wake him up, they hid all the documents again and grabbed their pistols, off they go. Using their military training they circled around the house from the side, Gordon was sitting on his porch with a high-powered rifle, not willing to go quietly, he knew they were back but not sure which men. Gordon reflected on his past mistakes, what he did to his family, his comrades, and his country. To this point he was not sure what the motive was for these men chasing him down, was it the war? Or was he in full panic mode from the fear of being discovered? Gordon grew up in New Jersey in a modest family, he was always intrigued by war and enlisted as soon as he could. He got married before he left to fight but was not aware his wife was pregnant until she told him over the phone, he did not want children that early, but the baby was on its way. He made his way up the military ranks and led his first troops well before Tolson existed, his daughter is much older than the two privates chasing him down. He never had any remorse for his betrayal, nor did he care that he dragged his daughter into it, he was a stern military officer and even his children had to obey. Why pick Susan? She was the oldest and wisest of his children, her schoolwork was fantastic, she followed all the rules, and was willing to learn any subject matter, even espionage and treason. The Germans got to him early in the stages of WWI, he was overseas in Belgium at the time, they offered him money, protection for his family, and housing. He was sworn to secrecy and the Germans changed his identification for him, he kept his American ID tags so he could get back home. In 1914 his Daughter had enlisted for a nurse in the Army, he used his connections to get her assigned to his troops. She thought it was to keep her safe, but her father had bigger plans and a vision as to how she could help. The best bait to trap a man is an attractive woman, Susan had it all and she would be the one to entrap any soldiers with the burning desire to be with a woman. The German set her up with a new identity once he told them his plan to use her for mass murders of soldiers, especially officers. She infiltrated officers' quarters first and put on a show of dancing and flirting with lap dances and kissing to start, their wives would never know, and all is fair in love and war!

CHAPTER 6

Susan had to learn to speak German or at least fake it with a broken accent, she learned quickly. She was trained in hand-to-hand combat, espionage techniques such as wire taps, and using every type of firearm available. The beginning was tough, she had punches, bruises, and torcher treatments, the same her father went through. The Germans had to make sure she would not break information to any enemies. She started with small jobs, pulling information from every American possible and relay to her father immediately, at times she would be gone for weeks, part of the job. One of her first assignments was to blow up the camp of Major Arthur Conrad, one of Americas finest officers, but he nor his troops saw this coming, these are the first one-hundred and fifteen men she killed. She circled the camp late at night, moving Ninja like through the camp dressed in all black and black face paint, she had gone undetected so far. Susan planted bombs around the camp so she could trap the soldiers without and escape route, once the ignited no man would be able to cross the flames if they survived the blast, she had a reserve of hand grenades for backup. The Americans were camped thirty miles from the German Western Front, they were stationed in Mount Blanc France. Their assignment was to keep marching toward the German border and once in position, open fire and take out every fox hole or German camp possible, no prisoners! Susan was one day ahead of them, courtesy of the other Germans or rat traders on the war, she was confident, calm, and really enjoyed what she was doing, a sick mindset brought on by her insane father. When her plan was in place she began igniting the bombs as soldiers slept while others were on guard, they had no time to think of anything, within minutes they were all dead, she completed her mission. She even shot soldiers in the back if they somehow survived and tried to run for cover, she showed no mercy, she was thirsty for more blood. For her next mission she assassinated an American, General Walter Young. He was on the threshold of taking down German intelligence and rescuing POWs from the concentration camps, she would not let that happen. When he stopped taking a leak in the woods, she came up behind him and slit his throat ear to ear, she ran off through the woods to safety, he was found ten minutes later in a pool of blood. Her father ordered her back to his base camp for her safety, she was hidden in her own barracks underground, he would start plotting his next mission for her with his officers. She was not allowed to communicate with her mother or siblings, who would have to wait, and this is a secret they would take to their graves, her mom would have a heart attack if she knew what was going on. She was proud her daughter was serving the United States as a nurse, so she thought, if she did not get messages from the Army stating she was dead, her mom assumed every day she was alive. Susan would drop her telegrams occasionally, but no details just a hello and miss you. With all this going through her father' mind while sitting on the porch, he never saw them coming. Tolson shot him at direct range with a German Ruger and a silencer attached, the bullet passed through his brain immediately killing him. "What the hell did you do" questioned Whiteway, "why did you do that" Tolson whispered to keep his voice down and replied, "this is a man who cannot live, he will hurt the military and our country again." The two dragged the rugged dead body off the porch and threw him in one of the barn stalls. A trail of blood started on the porch and ended in the barn, his wife or Susan would surely find him the next morning. Next, they had to enter the house to look for her, one went in the back, one in the front, Whiteway took the upstairs to no avail, while Tolson struck out downstairs, she knew they were coming and did not care if her father died, she wanted to live and go away. She could live here or Germany, she had all her contacts there and passport and visa to travel, she was confident. They checked out back, the Rolls was there but the other truck was gone, she was on the move. She was headed southwest toward West Virginia, she knew the Shenandoah Mountains and its caves very well, she could throw them off that way. With no idea which direction she went or if she even left town, the two men are dejected they want this woman in the worst way to make her pay for her crimes. They go back to the room Whiteway rented out, Tolson was due back to Mary by 8 PM, he has not time to chase down Susan, they would need a train ride and still do not know which direction to go. Tolson looked at Whiteway and asked who he knew in other states, he remembered names from all over, they decided to split the territory. Tolson would head back to Michigan for now and contact comrades in Ohio, Illinois, Indiana, and Wisconsin. Whiteway would reach out to Virginia, West Virginia, Kentucky, North Carolina, and Tennessee. They agree to make sure the contacts are armed and know all about Susan, she is far from a pushover, she is capable of murder, it does not matter who it is. The two agree to talk Tuesday night, this will give them time to get replies from the telegrams, or the phone calls they made. On the ride back Tolson is struggling with his faith, he is not better than Susan, he just murdered her father in cold blood, regardless of his crimes, this is still murder. As he drove along, he saw a crate with what looked like animals moving around in it, not being sure what they were, he drew his weapon and approached. TO his surprise there were four dogs inside, poor little pups he thought, Tolson loved dogs, always had. He picked them up slowly and got them in the truck one at a time. He wrapped jackets and a blanket around them that was in the truck then stopped to get them food and water. The dogs were a Husky named Yaz, Snow, a Great Pyrenees, Colby, a Bichon, and Sophie, a Maltese, she is an older girl but as sweet as they come. Mary loved dogs around the farm so he was hoping they would help put a smile on her face. He got home past 8 o'clock and Mary had dinner for him, she was not upset but began pushing for answers. Tolson said "I have something for you Mary, come on outside" she could hardly believe her eyes, she was thrilled. They all ran to her licking her face, wanting their bellies scratched, and of course a snack, she grabbed potatoes and meat and put them in bowls. He promised to talk to her about it tomorrow night after dinner, right now he needed sleep as his Monday morning shift is fast approaching. He went to his room and decided to take a bath that night so he would sleep better, he made it a quick one and went back to his room. He had to decide how to tell Mary about all of this, how he saw her husband get shot in the head by a sniper and he knew it was Susan. He could not sleep so he dug deeper into more documents and found out she had wiped out another unit of soldiers at Charleroi as they were ready to cross into Germany from Belgium, her father was disguised as an American officer in charge. He always had his uniform and all credentials with him, he was not sure which side he would have to jump onto to survive, the spy world is untrustworthy. Her father had spies in his American camp, they helped Susan plant bombs all around the camp and stole whatever firearms they could take to leave soldiers defenseless. The spies lined bombs and dynamite all around the camp, in jeeps and trucks, and to trees, this will surely crush all the soldiers and the camp. They reeled back the detonator for the dynamite with the wicks, they just had to connect the live wire to the end terminal and boom, mission complete. Susan was the ringleader, and her first goal was to clear her father and mentor from the camp, he slithered off like a snake to safety; once he was in the German tank and heading to a new site, she gave the order. The camp and skies lit up like the Fourth of July, within fifteen minutes, two-hundred and fourteen Americans were dead, not one left breathing, she smiled with enthusiasm as if he were proud, and he was indeed. Her death toll was now at three-hundred and sixty-four, her own blood, the country that gave her family opportunity, was no longer important to her. She could kill people and go to sleep at night, a dark soul lived inside her.

CHAPTER 7

Monday morning Riley bumped into Tolson as he entered the shop, his hair was a mess, bags under his eyes, and his eyeballs were as red as a fire engine. "What the hell happened to you" he laughed, it is a long story my friend, Barry replied, "we will catch up at lunch." The morning was dragging so slowly as if he had a bag of concrete on his back, Tolson was impatient and could not wait to talk to Whiteway tomorrow night, it was only Monday at lunch! Riley and Tolson took the far bench outside to discuss what had happened over the weekend, Riley was floored with what he heard. He was stunned to hear about then number of soldiers slaughtered and even more so that Tolson cold bloodily killed a man, they were not in the military anymore, so this is not a casualty of war. Tolson snapped back, "do not judge me, I did what was right, he was, and still is military when this all happened," his crazy daughter is out there." Riley questioned where she went, we have no idea Tolson stated, no idea. He showed him the breakdown on paper, Riley wanted in bad just like Whiteway, they are growing in numbers and there are more out there willing to help catch this woman. Riley offered to reach out to people in New York, Maryland, and Delaware in case she stopped there, he also made a call to a senator he met in Connecticut. With the areas being covered they should have a good shot at finding her, they will meet at Tolson's tomorrow at 7 PM and call Whiteway and update each other's progress. Mary interrupted with a knock on the wall and wondered who his friend was, this is Private Riley, we served together. Mary wanted to let them know there was fresh coffee and ham sandwiches on the table, feel free to enjoy, goodnight. Tuesday morning the men got up to walk and feed the dogs, they needed exercise and play time after being locked in a crate. They assisted with chores on the farm and were ready to walk to work. Mary made sure they had food for the day, both men were so gracious they kissed her cheeks, and she blushed with happiness. The two men got home and went right to work on the farm. Mary was grateful and offered to let Riley have his own room as another guest had left unexpectedly, he accepted the offer so they could work closely together and put this behind them. Mary and her team put together a fabulous feast for their hard work, all the diners benefited as she cooked roast beef, potatoes, carrots, rice, and a big beautiful homemade pumpkin pie with fresh pumpkin! and a cherry pie, freshly picked that afternoon. After dinner the guys went outside and discussed their strategy, they were waiting for Mary. She had been more than good to them, and they wanted to hide nothing from her, as much as it would hurt. Mary left cleanup to the staff, and she strolled outside with a pitcher of lemonade and glasses, it was time to find out what was going on. Tolson and Riley gave her the background on Susan, Tolson did not go into the fact he slept with her, nobody but Kriel figured that out and he was dead, just leave it alone and keep his name clear.

Riley delivered the big blow, they saw Mary's husband get shot and they knew the assailant, it was an ambush with a rifle, Mary choked up and tears rolled down her face. She never imagined something like this, soldiers die when they are attacked by enemies, not a single spy who is from America. She told the men her husband was proud of his country and had no regrets enlisting and shipping out, his father was a Major in the Revolutionary War, the blood runs in the family. Mary sighed and asked how she penetrated through all these camps and soldiers, which is what they are trained to do, Riley replied, they are sick people. We are going after her because we want her to face the charges, we have more proof than we need to accomplish this. Tolson already had in his mind, that one of them is going to kill her, he was determined for it to be him. She was not happy they were acting like hunters, they were no longer in the military, but they told her they were doing it, so no more soldiers are murdered by her or her affiliates. Tolson and Riley asked

Mary to keep quiet, there are more people involved than you think, and we do not know who they are just yet. The two men went back to the business area of Mary's house because it was more private, they did not want other guests overhearing details of their conversations. They got on the phone and called Whiteway, he was anxious with news he had received, Susan was spotted at a store near the border of West Virgina and Kentucky. She continued her path to the southwest, headed for Mexico Riley stated, why do not we call Sergeant Greenwall, he said he lives in Galveston, Texas. The phone was off the hook so they could all hear Riley call Greenwall, he knew him best. The guys still had their other friends keeping an eye out for her in surrounding states to stop her before she gets that far. Greenwall answered the phone with an abrasive who is this, it is ten o'clock at night! It is Private Riley Sir! Riley, you punk, how are you doing? I am good sir and here with Tolson and Whiteway, they helped me get out of Germany, hello gentlemen, "good evening, Sir," the private answered. Once he heard what they were doing and what was going on, he said he would make calls and watch the states, give me information. Tolson repeated her looks, the vehicle, and to make sure all men are armed, he told Greenwall about the three-hundred and sixty-four men she murdered and there may be more. He lost his mind, he was a tough Sergeant and if he got a hold of this girl, she would be dead, and nobody would know. He suggested no more phone calls, if she is around, she will be tapping lines which have already happened, that is why she is on the run. They would use only code when writing telegraphs or letters, if needed, they would take trains and meet in the middle of the country to discuss any progress. Greenwall said he will contact American Operatives to start landing in these different states to wrap this up. Riley and Tolson went to work the next morning, it was a gray, rainy day and the walk to work was not all pleasurable, Mary needed the truck for errands today.

While they were working, Greenwall made his contacts and people were on the move, he sent a telegraph in code to let them know. At lunchtime, the two were surprised when a teenage boy came up and handed them the wire, he was rewarded with a tip. They both read it silently, knowing the military codes, they knew things were going to happen faster with a Sergeant on their side, he had more contact than anyone they knew. After work they met up with Whiteway, he had gotten on a train to Michigan and was waiting at the boarding house foyer. The three could do nothing but wait for intel to come in, they had to narrow their search within a state or two, right now, she could be anywhere. Sergeant Greenwall sent them a pleasant surprise, a telegraph in code stating a citizen called in a robbery and an abandoned car in Louisville Kentucky, the identification pointed it to the other car at the house. "Yah, it is a 1919 Model T, NJ plate number 68572, do you know it"? Tolson jumped and said, yes, that is Susan's car at her father's house. He also stated to the sergeant that he killed Susan's father, he was a traitor, murdered, and scumbag just like her, but Greenwall knew all about him and was glad to hear that. I want you guys to sit tight until we get more, go to work, do not change your habits, I have a feeling you are being tracked as of now. They stopped all further correspondence outside the three of them, they opened their door to go out and smelled the wonderful aroma from the kitchen, time for chow boys. They went to help Mary bring the food out as they were grateful for her hospitality and kindness, they even helped the staff wash dishes after. There were only eight diners that night, Missy Thomas was dancing at the local speakeasy, so most men went out. When all the guests had left Mary asked how it was going, she never said a word because she was also concerned spies were stalking them. She knew about military coverts being married to Lieutenant Morris for years. With a motherly smile she gave them all a hug and peck on the cheek, "I expect you here for dinner every night, do not let me down." The went out for a couple of beers at the local bar across the street to wind down, none of them had patience but also know choice but to wait. As they enjoy unwinding, Greenwall's men are on the move, they ripped the car apart from top to bottom searching for any information. The men found phone bugs, explosives, clothing Tolson described Susan would be wearing, and addresses. Guns were stashed under the seat and in the glovebox, and a small crate that held ten grenades was in the back seat, what is she planning, it looks like she is still hell bent on murdering more now that a U.S. soldier down gunned her father. Susan had fled to the mountains of Kentucky, she had no intentions of being captured or shot, her plan is to contact her allies and get back to Germany, they would hide her and protect her for her service. She made her way to the base of the Appalachian Mountains, a gorgeous scenery with density, she could make her way to the northeast corner and backtrack toward New Jersey or

Pennsylvania. She was rougher looking now, being on the run from everyone will do that, she was tired, hungry, and dirty she was fading fast. She hiked for two miles and as she ascended a hill, she saw a campfire and a family surrounding it, forest rangers doing random checks so she would have to stay low and out of sight. Her hair was currently blonde thanks to a wig, so she threw dirt on her face and entered their camp with a .357 drawn and ready for use. The young son at nine years old was nearby so she grabbed him and threatened the family if they did not stay quiet, "I will put a bullet in his head, I do not care"!! They all sat down, she tied up the father first, then the rest of the family and gagged them, all she wanted was food and water, towels, soap, and she took mom's shampoo to clean up when she got to a lake or a pond, it did not matter. She handed the little boy a knife and his father's watch and instructed him to wait twenty minutes then you can set your family free, the boy shook his head in agreement. As she trudged her way up the mountainside further, darkness fell upon her, and he was completely exhausted now. Susan would set up camp with the sleeping bag she took and make a small fire to heat up her food and coffee, she would bathe the next morning. The family that had been terrorized was now in their truck racing down toward the ranger station to report this maniac who was loose in the hills. Ranger Wilson was on duty, he immediately contacted local and state police, none of them had an idea with whom they were dealing. The next morning Susan awoke with a chill, the mountain temperature dropped to fifty degrees overnight, but she admired the beautiful skyline, The sun was peeking out over the top of the mountains and the sky was clear, wonderful day to make time. She was aware the family reported the raid, so she rushed to the lake, washed up nicely and removed the wig, she put on the new clothes she took from the camp and was ready to go. She made a small fire again and chowed breakfast and coffee, now she was running through the woods, she could hear faint dogs barking and police sirens. It did not mean they were close to her, but it was quiet in the morning. Susan was smart, when she left, she covered up all the camp area she made and set a fire south of the site, this would distract the posse. The fire rapidly expanded, it was big enough to halt the chase and get fire apparatus up to the site, a crop-dusting plane with water flew overhead to douse it the best they could. Susan laughed as she continued forward, but where would she go next? She must get to a town to use a phone, or hopefully a secluded farm so nobody sees her, she would hold another family captive, but she did not care about that. The state police called out to the Ohio and Virginia state police asking them to cover their side of the border, they gave a full description and notified them that she is armed and dangerous. As she turned south down the mountains she encountered three old timer hunters, they hear the news over the radio and demanded she stop and drop her weapon, she obliged as they were not aware of the .45 tucked into the back of her pants and the hunting knife that was strapped to her calf. They had her get on her knees and put her hands behind her back, a big mistake! One of the men walked up and said they should all have sex with her then turn her in, they all agreed. Whether it is the mountains or not, that is rape she said and would make sure they pay for it one way or the other, they had no idea what she meant by that. She looked at them and said okay, "I will let you do what you want to me right now," the first man approached with his pants down and she pulled her knife and cut his scrotum open, she had cut the ties binding her hands. She did not want a mess on her hands, but they asked for it, she pulled her .45 and put one dead center in both their foreheads killing them instantly, game over. She was aware the gunshots may have gained attention but hopeful the police would think they were hunters' rifles and not rush to the scene. Two days later she arrived at the base of the mountain near a large farm of about twenty acres, plenty of room to hide and more than enough food, water, and essentials, she had to find out how many people were there before entering the house or the barn. She got to the barn roof and took notice of six men out in the fields, they were not a threat as they were out at least one acre away from her. The state police would be coming to the area, she must act fast or be caught, she decided to go to the side door as it was screened in and unlocked. As she enters the home she can smell food from the kitchen, there is at least one or two people downstairs, the spiral staircase leading upstairs was creaking, meaning someone was heading down the stairs, she hid behind the sofa and waited. From her spot she could see them all at the same table for breakfast, a perfect opportunity, the guys in the fields ate earlier so they could get to work. As she approached the dining area the old floors creaked causing everyone to turn around, she told them she was there for supplies only and did not want to hurt any of them. The Robinson family told her to take what she needed but please do not hurt anyone, she told them she must make a call as well and needs privacy. The little girl pointed to the phone on the kitchen wall, they would only hear whispering from there, she could talk freely to her allies. Susan warned them that she had no problem hurting anyone so shut the hell up while she called. She ordered two girls into the kitchen to pack up food and water for her and she wanted a new shirt, and one hundred dollars that was it. She ordered the oldest son to get a shotgun off the rack and wanted a full box of ammunition then keys for one of the trucks that already has a full tank of gas. She called into Derk Schwizer, a colonel in the German army, he was the one to make things happen, he instructed her to turn South again and head toward North Carolina, he would meet her there. He would send a wire in code so she would know where to meet him, he would be in a town near East Durham. Her instructions were to pick up her telegram there and then proceed to the town he listed in the code. She came out of the kitchen and all the items she asked for were in the truck, no tricks, this family was not going to risk their lives. She ran out of the house, hopped in the truck and off she went, Mr. Robinson immediately called the local sheriff and told him the story and the direction she was heading and the plate number of his truck, T32-682. Susan was not fooled, she knew he would call the second she left, she abandoned the truck and stole a car out of another yard, freedom was near, but it was a long haul to her next stop. The sheriff found the abandoned truck and followed the tire tracks left by the car. He accelerated and was on the move, he used his radio to call into dispatch to send help. I am heading east past the old Northfork Stone building, tell all cars to block off the Loudon Bridge and do not let her through, shoot to kill. As Susan raced for the border she saw a sign for the bridge two miles ahead, she was going to abandon the car, cut through the woods, and look for a new vehicle. When the sheriff arrived, he saw the car and knew she was gone, he called out and had the rangers notified and state police in all counties, somebody stop this crazy person. Susan knew she had to hide out for a while, she was too tired to keep going and the sun had been heating up, it was now three o'clock in the afternoon, she had no idea. It would take time for her to find a suitable place, the locals knew those mountains and she could not throw off her scent when the dogs arrived. She found a nice old tunnel on the hillside, it was dark and there were plenty of tree branches to drag over it, the pine would help throw the dogs off. She cut a piece of her shirt and pants as she ran, tying them to different trees away from her spot, she jumped into a pond to wash off the scent as well. She put on her new shirt which belonged to the Robinsons, this would certainly keep the dogs away. She barricaded herself in and sat back until she could hear the noise of the posse go away, she laid down to sleep exhausted from the exercise and heat. She set a trap in the branches that would go off if they got close to her, it was nothing special just a stick holding in rocks that would collapse and keep them away from her. The posse came up within fifteen feet of her, but all her tactics worked, the dogs did not approach, and she heard them all go down the hill, she will have to track the footsteps, so she does not run into them later. For now, she would sleep and rest up for the morning hike and search for a new vehicle. Susan realized she had crossed the bridge so that was one obstacle gone, she awoke at five o'clock the next morning and started down the hill. She was hungry again, so it was time to find food as well. It will be a long day, but she is thinking she can make it to North Carolina tonight. While running, she trips and bangs up her leg and shoulder, this will slow her down and she knows it, she must get a car. With no map she does not know how far a town is but at the bottom of the mountain she smells food, there is a local diner about six hundred feet from her. Susan puts a plan in place to get over there, she will have to go to the back and get food from there. She may have to change her course and head north.

Silent Are The Five Hundred

CHAPTER 8

Back at the inn, the guys are working hard for Mary to keep the farm in order, they have not heard from Sergeant Greenwall yet and their patience is wearing thin. They talked about heading south out of Michigan but that would certainly put them in the hot seat with the sergeant! The men do not even know if he is on the way up here or who is in place chasing Susan, there are no updates to her location. Several calls were made to local police, sheriff offices as well as state police with minimal answers, until they reached a ten-year veteran with the Virginia State Police, Carl Radcliff. He was not supposed to give out any information, but he wanted to play a significant role in capturing her. He was smart enough to know all these law enforcement agencies would not be looking for someone who stole cookies from grandma's kitchen! When Greenwall reached him, he asked if he could mention his name to some soldiers he is working with, Radcliff complied and told him he wants in on the big chase.

He told Greenwall that he knows her name is Susan, and she has something to do with espionage where she killed Americans, his brother was killed in the war, and he wanted revenge. Carl had read the papers every day and watched closely. A local reported slipped by releasing her last known location, how she was dressed and even notated some of the evidence. Then another shocker in this story, Carl replied, "she is my distant cousin, have not seen her in years but I can help you. Greenwall answered sternly, "you do what I tell you to do, or I will have you shot, and I do not care if I am being taped, Carl agreed to take orders and action, he wants her off the streets, or preferably dead! "Okay stated the sergeant, I am sending my guys a message, once I hear back you will receive a telegram from one of them, code word is "Georgia" to throw off the hunters. Radcliff was excited to be part of a military operation, he had never served his country, but he was going to now, he did not need a medal or his name in the newspaper, he just wanted what he deemed justice. I took two days for Greenwall to get back to Carl, when he picked up the phone the sergeant simply said "Georgia" meaning he will see a telegram today from one of his men and he is to follow the instructions. Before Carl could say anything, the phone was slammed down on Greenwall's end, which was a reminder to pretend this call never happened. At 4PM right after work, Tolson headed down to the telegraph office with his friends to send off a message, he got one from Greenwall while at work again. He relayed a message to the clerk, "Georgia says to say hello, please return the message so we can connect somewhere," Don Tolson. They ask the clerk to have a kid run it over to them at the inn when it arrives, if they are not home try checking the bar. It has been one week since Susan was last tracked, there were no reports of seeing her, crimes or murders she could be tracked to, so what is she up to? Where is she? And what should they expect next, nobody has a clue, but they are getting close. Saturday morning brough more news that Susan was now heading up north, a message confirmed by the military squadron out looking, she had last been spotted near Philadelphia the night before. Carl Radcliff had retuned a coded message to "Georgia" stating he was coming to visit his grandmother and would like to see them, all in code of course so it confused the clerk. Radcliff left Kentucky soon after that on his way to meet the guys in Michigan. The plan was to leave his car near the Indiana border, take the plates off, burn it and get a train ticket. His drive was a long one, it is approximately four hours to the Indiana state line, and another five hours to Dearborn, but the train would get him there inconspicuously. By the next Tuesday they had not heard from Radcliff and notified Greenwall, he put some men on it right away to find him. On Thursday the boys in Michigan got a return message, Radcliff was found dead with two bullets in his heart, the work of Susan certainly! He was found slain on the side of the road like a wild animal, she even took his wallet, gun, and any documents in the car, she left the car as it was an easy target to spot her. Greenwall and his other men were heading north, they warned the guys to always be alert, take turns sleeping even in your room at the inn, never go anywhere alone. Susan is somewhere within one hundred miles of your area now; her mission is to create more disasters before she gets to Germany. Ever since Susan contacted her colonel Schwizer she knew exactly what was going on, every telegram, phone, radio, car was bugged, and they were tracking. Riley and Whiteway were working on Mary's truck Sunday when they noticed two small discs inside the vehicle, tracking devices, they pulled them off and brought them inside. Tolson arrived from the telegraph office and advised the men that Susan had killed the Kentucky trooper, she knows about all of us. We need to move from the inn and find cover in a haven, where would they find such a place? They sat with Mary and gave her all the gruesome updates, she was saddened to hear this, it meant she was not safe either, Susan would hunt her down for information about us. Mary was as stoic as a rock and she would not back away, she was well equipped with guns and knew how to use them. She had gone hunting and target practicing but never a person, she could do it if pushed against the wall. The guys moved Mary to the back of the inn, her room was in between all three of them so she felt safe, Tolson took first watch. Since Riley did not work at Ford, he would be around Mary all day to watch out for her, he would get the most sleep at night. Mary asked Riley to go over to the Johnson's farm for some wheat and flour, the stores were backordered, and she wanted the best. Riley put up his best fight with her and begged her to come with him, "I am fine" she stated, all the help is here, and Ralph has a shotgun, he was Mary's right-hand man on the farm for the last five years. Riley stopped on the way out and asked him to go on the porch with the gun and keep a close eye out, she means the world to us as she does to you. "yes sir" he replied,

I will take care of her. Riley was not gone long, fifteen minutes, he was glad to see Ralph still on the porch with the shotgun and the homecooked food smell from the kitchen. He dropped off the supplies to Mary and poured them into jars so she could use what she wanted; the rest went to the barn. When Tolson and Whiteway returned from work they cleaned up and ate an early dinner, Mary had no problem cooking twice for all they do and the protection they provide. She was not about to close her inn and run for it, she had pride and respect for her family and the work they all did building this place up. After dinner they went outside to talk about guarding the house and barn, if Susan breaks one entry point, it will be trouble for all. They wondered how much longer it would take for the back-up to arrive. They laughed about being afraid of one woman, what would it take to catch her and bring her down for good? There was an eerie still about the night, not one sound from the animals, the town, or the church bells, their concern raised through the roof.

Tolson commanded all to grab some guns, at least two each and assigned the guard posts. Riley, you take the rear of the house, Whiteway you have the rear of the barn, Ralph you take the porch again and I will watch the front and side of the barn. She is sneaky and will be in dark clothing, listen for sounds, do not look for a body, we will know when she is here. Remember she is heavily armed and well versed in combat, yell out if you find her and shoot her in the head, do not take chances. The night got later and darker and around 1 o'clock in the morning they heard a sound behind the barn, two took the sides and two took the front and back with guns drawn ready to fire. False alarm, a neighbor's cat started jumping around in the barn looking for mice, but it was a good reflexive drill for the men. Three days had passed since they heard from Sergeant Greenwall, the concern grew, last word they had he was on his way up with four specialized soldiers, relief they needed. Could be road issues Riley said, we need to stop worrying about everyone, "look what happened to Trooper Radcliff" stated Tolson, do not tell me not to worry. The night passes into morning without fault, if Susan is around, she is taking her time and tormenting them all. Sad news comes vis the newspaper the next morning, Greenwall and his associates made it to Springfield, Illinois, when they came out of dinner, they were gunned down in the street as if it were 1850. All five of them are dead, now what? Where can we find more contacts in the military? Tolson, Riley, and Whiteway were sick of waiting for Susan to show herself, "we need to take action" said Whiteway, it is time to hunt her, why are we waiting to be victims? All three agreed to go after her, first they had to gather all their intel and make sure they would head in the right direction, Tolson still had vibes she was nearby. When they all awoke the next day they had a sickening feeling, Mary was crying downstairs, they ran to her rescue. She was shaking terribly and said, "look outside, just look, it is awful." As they look over the land, they see cows slaughtered, one of her hogs was dead, and there was a family of rabbits cut to pieces. The men ran out and noticed a note on the barn door, it stated the following "I know you are after me and will not stop, but I will be in Germany by the time you find me, hi Tolson, how is it hanging? What does that mean shouted Riley, "How does she know your name? where have you seen her, and do not lie to us, she would have written all our names if the Germans told her. He hung his head and said, "I cannot tell you; Kriel told me to keep it to myself, I am sorry guys." But Riley was not accepting that and slammed Tolson against the barn wall, what is going on Don? We are your comrades and friends, do not hold out on us! Tolson teared up and babbled "I am a good soldier and leader, I loved my troops," but I screwed Susan but before I knew who she was, Riley slugged him in the face anyway and called him a loser. Whiteway looked like a kid at Christmas who did not get the bike he wanted, "what you could not have told us earlier? They calmed down and figured the past is the past, tell Mary we are going to the bar, we will be back around ten p.m. The boys came back to the inn a bit rowdy, which stirred the house and Mary woke up, she came out with a shotgun but quickly realized it was them. She got upset and pointed the gun at Tolson, "what was all the yelling about earlier, and what of you and this slut Susan"? Tolson told her the entire story, he was not proud or happy about it, she tried to understand but then slapped him across the face and told him to sleep in the barn tonight so she could cool off! An hour later Mary walked out to the barn with a couple of cold beers, nobody knew she liked beer, but it was a hot night, she handed one to Tolson and said, "let's talk." They spent forty minutes discussing her husband and his career, then asked him why he joined the military. I wanted to help my country with dignity and honor, to fight for our land and progress, but I certainly screwed some of that up. Are you part of the reason my husband was assassinated? No, I had nothing to do with spies or setting up soldiers to die, I would never betray my officers or troops like that. Tolson stated she was just sex, drugs, and alcohol, I had no idea who she was. Mary sat back and looked at his eyes, she was great at reading eyes and eyes are the windows to the soul and told him she believed him. She asked him about the war, he went into details making sure to skirt around her husband and issues that may make her angry or sad. He told her that all the officers and soldiers respected Lieutenant James Morris, we would have died for him, he was an honorable man and soldier. She gave him a hug and told him to go into his room, tomorrow is a new day, tonight is the past, "Thank You Don for opening up with me." The next morning was Saturday already, the men ate and went out to clean up the mess. They would carefully carve the cow for the meat and the pigs were good for bacon, ham, and a pig roast! When they had finished picking up the catastrophe, they heard five or six shots in the house, grabbed their guns and ran inside. Another mess, "no Mary no" screamed Tolson as he took a slug in his right arm, Riley and Whiteway began firing, but they were not sure where the shot came from. Mary and her staff had been gunned down in cold blood, that whore Susan the bitch is here, kill her!!! Mary's left ear was cut off, a message from Susan that she is vicious and will take any torture to extremes, the doctor stated it happened before she was killed. The other bodies lay slumped over each other in a pile of blood, they sorted them one at a time for positive identification, in total, six were dead. They searched the barn, house, fields, no Susan, what? there were no cars, no plane taking off, no motorized vehicle sounds anywhere, how did she get out? Riley grabs a truck "I need to go to the doctor" Tolson shouted then we will find that bitch and burn her at the stake! I have had enough of her killing sprees. Tolson is at the doctors for one hour getting the slug removed, clean the wound and stitch it closed. The entire town was up in arms over Mary and the others, a sick feeling came over them all, then a feeling of horror, is this woman still in town. The men helped clean up the bodies and get them to the morgue and assist with getting the funerals ready, something about which they were not excited. Mary was a mom to them, and the sweetest lady ever, besides his real mom of course. Mary's niece and nephew were only seventeen and fifteen, fortunately, they were at the church when this happened. The police came to do a full investigation of the property inside and out, the barn, attic, loft, rooftops, they went everywhere. Detective Michael Gray was leading the case, he was stunned at the scene. He had been a law officer for eighteen years now and never encountered anything like this, he excused himself and went outside to vomit and try to take this all in. He asked the officer inside to send out Tolson, Riley, and Whiteway immediately, there were a lot of pieces to the puzzle left unsolved, he needed answers. The men walked slowly to the detective; they all knew this was going to be a lengthy conversation but not at the farm. The detective told them to hop in the car, they were going to the police station to interrogate all three. Gray had the men separated in rooms with one office leading the conversation for each, they would take notes and compare. Tolson was with Gray, Whiteway with officer Jones, and Riley with officer Kent, all had reputations as bullies on the police force. Jones was six foot, four inches and weighed two-hundred and seventy pounds and a look that would kill a rattlesnake just by staring at it. Kent was only five foot eight inches but tough as steel, he was known for putting perps in the hospital before the jail cell. Tolson gave the entire story to Gray which took three hours, he covered every war detail regarding Susan and even told him about the sex upfront. He told him about the three hundred and twenty-nine American soldiers she murdered with her father, he could not divulge that he shot her father, it would be deemed an assassination in the law's eyes. Riley and Whiteway provided more details of the gore since they never met or had sex with Susan, they told the police she is a complete psycho and heavily armed and dangerous. They were both with their officers for over three hours, the police were trying to trip them up and make sure they had nothing to do with the killings. For the next two hours the ex-soldiers were asked to give their life stories to the police, where they lived, parents' names, siblings, jobs and if they had weapons from the military. They all admitted to having weapons and using them trying to catch Susan, the men told the officers where their guns were at the inn. He sent an officer to go collect them all and bring them back, even though her father was killed in another state, Tolson was smart enough to not tell them about that one. The men were locked up for protective custody, the last thing Dearborn police want is a vigilante gang of three running around angry looking for a woman to kill. They all made it clear they will kill her when they find her, Gray and his officers had no problem with that in their minds, they were all veterans as well, but they could never speak it with the badge on their shirts. The men were brought food as it was a long day of questioning, the morning could not be here soon enough, they wanted to be on the streets.

CHAPTER 9

Tolson had been missing his mom and she was overly concerned, she had not received a call or telegram in over three weeks, he must be busy she thought. To her surprise Tolson called that night to catch up with her and the siblings. He talked mostly about Ford trying to avoid any open conversations about the reality of today, but she had some news for him as well. He continued about Mary and the inn, how wonderful she was and how she treated people, then he told her what happened, his mom began to cry and turned pale. He went on to tell her about Susan, the war, and his relationship with her, mom was astounded once again. "You left your troops to be with a woman, what kind of soldier were you"? before he could answer he got mom's working hands across his face, it stung, and she did it again. Your father would never have done that, but it is too late for that speech, anything else you want to tell me? Tolson advised his mom that this is the entire story, and it is true, the police and ex-soldiers are looking for her, she is dangerous. His mom spoke up and said she would move on from this, but there is much she would have to tell him, they had been on the phone for over an hour with her son's story, so they agreed to talk again tomorrow right after work. Tolson went back to the bar to meet up with the others, they could use some beer and whiskey tonight. They shared the details of the conversation with the police and got back to Susan, where is she? Tolson asked if they had found any added information or contacts we can have help, the others are dead. Riley piped up, "I contacted Sergeant Conrad from Florida, he is offering his help and taking a train to get here tomorrow night" He is rounding up any other ex-soldiers he can find, and he also has a friend on their police department, they will all be here. The three spent the night going over Susan's moves through the country, trying to narrow down to where she would be now, but Whiteway insisted she was local, no more than fifty miles from us. The next day while

Tolson and Whiteway were at work, Riley cranked up Mary's truck and started searching. Up and down country roads, local routes, highways, and even went into bars, shops, offices, and schools with Susan's photo asking everyone if they had seen her. He hit a home run with Nancy Reynolds, a typist at the Morgan Henry Company, they sell insurance. Nancy stated she saw a woman that looked like Susan but not an exact match, "where did you see her" asked Riley. I went for a haircut the other day and she was in the salon; her picture was not posted until the next day then I realized it was her. She was wearing blue pants with a gray shirt and what looked to be army boots, and she looked exhausted. Riley asked about her purpose being there, she got a haircut and asked them to darken her here with henna, so her hair is dark now. Riley could not thank her enough and sped back to the inn and waited patiently for his friends to get home from work. Meanwhile he still checked the map of Susan's movement and dug deeper into documents, there was one he came across that they had not talked about, it was folded in between the bag compartment and a postcard. He was dumbfounded but could not wait to talk to his friends, they would certainly be upset. When they got home, Tolson headed for the phone to follow up with his mother as promised, Riley barked and demanded he hear this before he calls his mom, he agreed. The paper he found listed addresses of Susan's relatives from Massachusetts to California and everyone in between, they must expand their network across the country. The three wonder how she got to be so elusive and why this is taking so long with limited information, Tolson stops them in mid-sentence and said "Kriel and I found an identification tag with Cedar Rapids Iowa, Riley you are from Iowa, can you make some calls? Riley went to Mary's old office, grabbed his phone book, and began making calls, Susan could be as far as Colorado and Whiteway had family there. Riley made over one dozen calls and produced three willing to get involved, he told them they would receive a telegram in code and pictures of Susan would be mailed through the United States Postal Service. He directed them to call as soon as they received everything. Whiteway reached out to his wife and father in Colorado to alert them, she has a talent for finding family members with different last names or identifications, telling his father to always carry a gun, I Love you. They planned to leave tomorrow for Troy Michigan and casually check out the streets and businesses in hopes of finding Susan, this had gone on too long, and it was time to finish it. Tolson excused himself to go call his mom, he would be back. Mom picked up the phone and her voice was shaken and scared she was never the type to get nervous, he asked what was going on. She stated that a letter arrived from a friend of his yesterday, it was left on the doorstep not delivered with the mail. "Have you opened it" he asked, not yet I was waiting for you to call. When she opened the letter she became more on edge, read it to me mom, come on! The letter was only a paragraph long." Dear Donald Tolson, how are you doing today"? I am writing to you regarding all your dead friends, soldiers or not. You have been trying to track me down and with not much luck I might add, you will not find me, ever. I enjoyed killing Mary because she was so close to you, who else is that close to you Private"? "I will get you before I leave this country and you will hunt me no more, the same for your friends. Love Susan, you idiot" Without hesitation Tolson tells her to get anyone in the house, hop in your car, and head for Michigan, stay with me so you are safe, Please mom! She did not want to argue with him, she agreed to do so after they packed clothes and essentials, they would be on their way, he would call back in ten minutes to make sure she was okay and leaving. He called back, the car was packed, and they were leaving, she even called from another place so she could get out of the house faster. Riley's contacts got back to him that night, no luck. They searched everywhere including the two addresses Tolson gave him, she was not in town. Whiteway bombed too, no luck from his team out looking for her, they left pictures with local authorities. Tolson figured his family would arrive about 9 AM and they prepared their rooms, Mary's family was happy to have them. When they arrived the ground rules were set, no going anywhere without someone accompanying you, home before dark, and all doors locked by 7 PM. Down to a nice dinner at Mary's dining room, the mood was somber knowing how their friend died, but the banter kept their minds busy. Mom wanted to know all about Whiteway and Riley, so it was a long night of conversation. She pushed them to see what they knew about Tolson's activities with Susan, they knew nothing, she ended the conversation.

CHAPTER 10

It was a hard night of drinking for three friends so much that they slept until 11 A.M., mom did not want to wake them. They struggled to the kitchen where coffee was waiting, the staff asked what they would like to eat, "lots of everything Tolson yelled out, please." The men decided las tonight to not call anymore contacts, there is too much involvement and too many hands in the cookie jar, we must stop. Then Whiteway asked about the Florida team, they are still on the way here, what do we do with them? Detective Gray walked in at that moment and said, "you will do nothing, they are all dead"! He took a seat, and mom made him breakfast as he began to explain the situation with this posse as he called it, more like a lynch mob. They were near the Indiana border when their car blew up, anybody in the area thought it was flat tires or a backfire, but upon investigation it was a rocket launcher that killed them all. I want you boys to understand this is my town, not yours and I uphold the laws in the book, do not let me catch you firing rounds at anyone, even if it is Susan. Susan had made her way just north of Dearborn, tucked away in the woods with minimal shelter and food, she designed a lean too so she could sleep and hide, Whiteway was correct, she stayed in the area. The men did not know that however and began to wonder if they could catch her, at some point she will try to get to Germany. Susan was doing planning of her own in her haven, she would rob the bank, steal food and a car, and head to the Canadian border, it will be easier to cross from there. She had several contacts there and would get whatever she needed, including flights. What the town does not know is she has been watching them, what time businesses open, how late people are in town, where the police spend time together, and what the bank hours are. If she can make her way back down when it is light, she can strike tonight when everyone is inside or asleep. Susan can operate any vehicle so stealing a car is easy, the other plans will be more difficult, but she is a seasoned spy and tough.

She got halfway down the mountain and the chill was setting in, she decided to build a fire and head down later, she was warm but hungry so she would not wait too long. Susan got into town about 9 P.M., all was quiet as she suspected and made her way to the rear of the bank. She was able to bore in the lower wall and crawl through it to the basement, she was not upstairs, so no alarms rang, smart chick! She filled a duffel bag with three thousand dollars, she was not sure of her exact plan to get out of the country, but she would need money for everything. Her next mission was to take a car, she chose a 1916 Chevrolet 490 Touring car for comfort, and it was old enough to not draw attention to, people love flashy new vehicles. With the duffle bag in back it is time to go food "shopping" or shoplifting, she needed a lot of things including matches for campfires, coffee, and bread. If she had not time to cook on a fire, the bread would keep her full for a long time, she again quietly snuck in the back of the store and began shopping. When she was done, she looked outside to make sure things were still quiet in town, all was good as far as she could tell. As she packed the car, she thought she heard something around the front, so she drew her weapon and went cautiously to check it out, as she reached that point, a shot rang out and she fell. Susan had been spotted by an undercover police officer and he knew all about her bullshit and would take no chance with his own life. The bullet struck her right shoulder, she knew she had to get to the car and screw out of town, the police officer followed her to the alley with his flashlight and gun drawn, he wanted to get the cuffs on her, but it was dark back there. She had already run around the building to the right and was now behind the officer and he sensed it, he was about to die. She told him to drop his weapon and hands against the car, he complied, she came up behind him and slit his throat ear to ear, a gunshot would have brought more police. She put his body in the back of the car and dumped him in the lake heading out of town, nobody would find him, they would think he was missing or abandoned his family and job. Susan swung by the apothecary to grab medical supplies. She drove up Mountain Valley Road and hid the vehicle in the woods, she still wanted to stay around determined to get Tolson and the crew. But now she was injured and even as tough as she was, she needed to repair the wound and get some sleep, she would be hurting tomorrow. The small fire she had built was perfect, low-flame, minimal smoke so she would not be detected, as it was, she was protected under the dark skies with the time approaching midnight. Her medical experience was extensive as well, she removed her shirt and bra and dug into the wound with a knife she heated up. She had to pull the bullet out without cutting or damaging more tissues, it hurt like hell, but she did it, the bullet came out and she began to bleed quickly. She threw some iodine and whiskey on it and held a wad of cotton cloth over it from the pharmacy. She put the thread into the needle and began sewing, it was painful, so she picked up a small stick and bit it down. She washed the wound off with alcohol one more time and began stitching, her hands were steady which made it a tighter stitch, it took her under ten minutes, a total of fourteen stitches. The way she was standing when she was hit allowed her to miss a direct shot in the shoulder, therefore the wound was not as big as she thought. It was enough to slow her down, she was weak as she lost plenty of blood and fading fast, time for bed. Her camp had limbs of trees and leaves and whatever else made her a pseudo sleeping cot and kept her hidden from the elements and police! She was too tired to cook, a piece of bread and her eyes were closed, she would not wake up the same person. Morning came fast for her, she was dizzy, blood was leaking from the bandage, and she could not move her shoulder, it was as if someone were sitting on it, so she hung it by her side and started moving around. Susan threw some breakfast together, stuffed it into the bread like a sandwich, grabbed her gear, and headed toward the car. She tripped and rolled about fifty feet down the mountainside hitting all her bones on the rocks, trees, and other debris, she yelled in pain. Worried that there may be hunters or explorers in the woods, she got up, ignored the pain, and got to the hidden car; she climbed in the back and would rest for two hours. She could hear voices but did not know the direction or what they were saying, either way, they were coming for her, she was sure of it. The voices passed but she would remain there longer than she wanted, the risk was too high with the injury, as it was, she had to now shoot left-handed, but she is a righty. Back in town the three soldiers were stumped, they had no idea where to look for her, but they agreed the mountains would be best, a needle in the haystack search, but must start somewhere. They drove to Mountain Valley Road, the access road Susan used, it would give them the best view to spot anything out of the ordinary. They drove to a cut out and parked, there were three paths at the site, each man would take one and call out if they find anything. They thought about using radios, but there was too much noise. Detective Gray ended up at the inn, he began questioning everyone on where the three men went, someone had to know something. Nobody had any idea, they left early without leaving a note, but they did mention Mary's truck was gone, the farm truck. Gray shook his head in disgust and fear, fear for the men's lives and fear for his town. As he turned to leave an explosion crashed into the inn, Tolson's family, Gray, and Mary's staff were dead, another awful turn of events, it was Susan of course. She told Tolson she would get him, and those he loved, another promise kept. The men heard the explosion from the mountain and ran to the truck and sped home, when they got there, the inn was nearly burnt down, and they saw no bodies outside. Son of a bitch Tolson screamed as he ran, there is no way anyone survived this! They all expected, and knew the worst before nearing the house, there was no way they could enter, debris was everywhere, and the fire was still going strong. Tolson dropped to his knees crying and screaming "why God, why," his friends tried to console him but to no avail, his family was butchered. The fire department showed up with the police quickly behind them, they knew Detective Gray was dead, his car stood idling as he only expected to be in the house for a couple minutes. The firemen do their best to control and douse the fire as humanly possible, the men jumped in to drag bodies out and help with the fire, Tolson grabbed his mother first, a scene that will never leave his mind. Her burns were so extensive, he could not make out her face the way she was before. As he looked over her, he saw the bracelet his grandpa Tolson had gotten her before he left the family, that was his positive identification, again he had to put a beautiful mother six feet under in the ground. Whiteway and Riley had nothing to say, what could they? They consoled him the best they could by holding him up and getting him away from the house and bodies, he was not able to stand on his own. He planned to bury them back home in Illinois, he would need the help of his friends to get them there. Riley interrupted and said, "I mean no disrespect, but why don't we bury them here, on Mary's farm." "No, I have to bring them home, we have family back there and they need to find out, I have calls to make." After forty-five minutes on the phone, he reached the relatives and asked others to reach out to the next family members he needed help with, it was another long, sad night for the men. The next day was full of making plans to get the bodies home; his mother, two sisters, and two cousins had arrived with the group. The staff's families asked the men to help them bury their bodies and they agreed, it was a morbid Saturday afternoon, the dark skies and rain made it no more pleasant. Riley and Tolson talked, and they were no longer going to work at Ford. They arrived Monday morning and notified them, the foreman expected it with all that keeps happening. The plant had already lost fifteen employees who moved out of states when this onslaught began, what's three more he joked. In all seriousness he came back and told the men that it was a pleasure having them here and he gave Tolson a handshake and a hug, he had lost all his family, his heart had been ripped out of his chest and the foreman knew it. He excused himself to get their final pay and offered his assistance in any way to help them, but he knew they were going on a mission, and he could not leave his family and risk dying. The walk back to town seemed to last for days, they swung by the new hotel and got Whiteway for some drinks, they would keep themselves from getting drunk this time. After Mary's house blew up the owner of the Pavilion Hotel offered them a free stay, they graciously accepted and did work to earn their rooms. While they drank the topic of giving up the hunt for Susan came up, the thought sickened them all, but how much longer could this last? They have all contributed in ways that go beyond friendship, unfortunately, all the people they dragged into this mess are dead, there will be no more calls reaching out for help. All three are exhausted, weak, and feel defeated because Susan is still on the run and headed to freedom, once in Germany, she would be untouchable! Riley disagreed with giving up or contacting people, "why not call the Royal Mounted Police in Canada and alert them to guard the border," the room fell silent, there was no interest. Tolson piped up by adding that he lost his entire family, he was burnt out and had no soul left to chase her down, he began to weep. To catch her they would have to watch airports, hotels, highways, and the dreaded woods, acres and acres of trees and brush. Whiteway suggested getting sleep, it was now 10 PM and we can re-evaluate tomorrow, sounds good said Riley, let's go. They awoke Thursday morning with fresh minds, after a huge breakfast and coffee, they walked to the police station to see if they had created any leads. The policemen would not give them the time of day, enough happened with crimes in their small world, "why don't you call on more of your Army friends so they can die too." Tolson wound up and smashed the desk sergeant in the mouth, assaulting a police officer is a huge crime, but the sergeant let it go considering what Tolson lost. He ordered them to get out and it was over, no more law enforcement questions would be answered, not in Dearborn anyway. It was time for them to move on to a new town, their welcome had worn out and there was a stale smell in the air which reminded them of dead bodies. Back at the hotel they collect their belongings, check in with the owner and give him Thanks for everything he has done for them. When the men arrived at the train station they had a big problem, "where the hell are we going, there was no decision yet" Tolson spoke up in a weak voice. Several cities came up in conversation, each one bringing them closer to the Canadian border, but there had been no confirmation Susan was headed there, purely speculation from the contacts they used to have. Riley suggested going to Lansing Michigan, just one and a half hours away, he still suspects Susan is in the Dearborn area and this will keep us close to her. An agreement was made, it was the right choice, they got in the truck and headed out to their new spot. When they arrived, it was as if they were movie stars, the news was all over the state of Michigan. The locals paid close attention to the three as they parked and walked over to the Border Hotel, the name came from being two hundred and seventy-five miles from Canada.

CHAPTER 11

The newsroom editor came over to the hotel and asked for an interview, we may be able to help if you publicize this from your side of the story. Nobody replied except Tolson, "we will think about it and let you know tomorrow, for now, stay quiet or you may get hurt." The editor walked away frightened and upset, Tolson felt bad and ran outside after him and made him stop. Sir, I did not mean to come across like that, but I lost my entire family through this, and I have had enough. The editor introduced himself as Edward Kane, he explained that two years earlier he lost his family in a car accident, a wife and three small children, so I do understand your pain. Kane was forty years old and built his business from the ground up, he was slightly overweight and walked with a bad limp, war injury. He battled alcoholism after his family's tragic death but was coming out of that dark cloud, he wore a long beard, and his face was covered with wrinkles. Tolson replied with how sorry he was, but they cannot be found by this person, she is insane and will kill again and you as the writer could be a target. Kane agreed to keep silent until they made up their minds about this. Let's grab coffee tomorrow Kane suggested, the four of us can review every aspect of the damage that may come from this, fair enough? Tolson agreed. Kane asked him to bring all the documents they had, it will help me understand better, Thank You. After breakfast Kane invited them to his office for privacy and to have enough room to lay out all the evidence. He asked them to use the rear side door to avoid any snoopers that try to come around while we meet. It was a nice cool day in Lansing, about seventy-five degrees and clear, with the sun smiling down on the town. Kane set up a story board just as if he were drafting an article, he lined the information by sequence of date as bet the men could now remember. The articles, photos, descriptions of Susan and even the piece of rag they retrieved from her shirt were all out in the open for them to view. Tolson began telling the story to Kane, from the day he met her in Germany to the moment they were all here talking. Riley and Whiteway joined in as there were just so many parts to the journey, Kane shook his head in shock when he heard the horrible slayings of all the people right from the horses' mouths. The meeting lasted eight hours, they were mentally exhausted and could no longer think, time to call it a night. Kane offered to let them stay at his house, but they declined based on putting him in harm's way, they would meet again tomorrow at his office. At 7 AM the men entered the building secretively again, turning their heads to make sure nobody saw them, the cost was clear. Kane was there already and put a "closed" sign on his door, the employees would think he was off for the day. He had thought about this all night and suggested to the men they publish a smaller article. His friends would publish it in another town, giving the advantage of keeping Susan off track. They would send Kane a copy of the article, which would feature a picture of

Susan and her ability to disguise herself and change languages, and most importantly DO NOT APPROACH, she is armed and dangerous! He was not sure how they would receive it; he was hoping for the best. The men thought it over for thirty or forty minutes covering the pros and cons of this, it really was a significant risk and could turn disastrous. They all wanted to capture her so what did they have to lose? All three agreed to do it, and Kane drafted the article so they could review it. From Susan's perspective she would love the attention and her notoriety of being an evil person, deceitful and deadly, in her sick mind she would cherish the story. The four reviewed the article, they read it aloud over one dozen times to make sure they heard it right and no details were left out. Riley pointed out that she had been shot, make sure we add that, Tolson suggested sending a telegraph in code. Bruce Merrill was his war friend, just like these three, he trusted him with his life and would understand code. Bruce's business was in Pittsburgh PA., far enough away to make her think they are still checking that area but hopes she will remain around Michigan long enough to be caught. The article described her as five foot six inches tall, dark, or blonde hair, American from New Jersey but speaks English, German, Italian, and French. She was military trained and a traitor, and should be considered extremely DANGEROUS, if seen, contact your local or state police, DO NOT attempt to apprehend. She is currently responsible for the murders of three hundred and seventy-nine American soldiers during WWI, and has assassinated over two dozen police, citizens, and ex-military here in our own country. It also included a picture of her with both hair colors, and a description of the last clothes she was seen wearing. That was it, not a full-length page, enough to get her attention with the goal of her making a big mistake. They can only wait until it hits all the papers in PA. Bruce sent back a telegram immediately stating he is on board and will get this done, it will be in tomorrow's 5 AM delivery trucks and plastered everywhere. When the article was released, people everywhere were up in arms. Keeping their kids home from school, purchasing a gun, and crowding police stations asking them what they were doing about this, the city had been upended. The next day reporters from all over the state and country flocked to Pittsburgh, pounding on the doors of Merrill's business demanding interviews and getting a peek at all the evidence on hand; of course it was all in Michigan. Merrill called Police Chief Mahoney and asked for help, seven reporters were arrested for causing public disorder, his business was now quiet, and he would let Kane and company know the stir it caused. They all had no doubt this was on the radio already as well; the country would be alerted by noon time. Merrill sent a messenger with another coded telegraph; it was his nephew, so he trusted him. It was sent within ten minutes and Kane was surprised when a messenger brought him the wire, they were happy nothing happened to him or his shop. Now the waiting game begins, where, if anywhere will she be spotted? The men go downtown to Poppy's pizza joint, keep it low key and they could hide in the back corner behind the bar where it is dark. Poppy himself came to tell them he has guards in front and back, they will get you home later as well. He was born and raised her and knew everyone, whether it was the law or against it, but they all respected him. He told them his men will follow them around and assure their safety. They were heavily armed, part of the Barozzi gang he grew up with, and already put a hit out on Susan for $100,000 without letting the guys know. Whiteway, Tolson, and Riley had no idea the size of the mob out looking for her, the own the streets so information would flow more freely when and if she comes out of hiding. Poppy cannot tell them because he would tie himself to the mob, even though the town knew it. They were aliens here and better off not knowing his business, Kane however grew up here and he was sworn to secrecy about the mob hit.

CHAPTER 12

Susan paid a kid two dollars to grab her a newspaper which he gladly did, she was currently hiding out in Flint, sixty miles from them, Riley was correct. She set up a small camp in the woods near a trailer park, a rundown old place at the back of the river. There were thirty mobile homes there, mostly older folks, so they would stay clear of trouble, she was not concerned. Susan set herself up behind a stone wall about ten feet tall, remnants of an old building, but it was a great shield from the world. She had plans to make and her situation was getting tougher with the media and the mob, although she did not know about the mob. Her wound was healing nicely, no infection or broken stitches, if she were a kind person she would make a good nurse. She got to build a fire to cook, she was hungry from the running and tired because her body was worn down. She went to the river, undressed, and washed herself up, she felt better now and more awake. As she began to cook, she wondered to herself if she is as tough as she had always been, peace and quiet makes her mind wander and question her abilities. She had plenty of weapons so defending herself would not be that difficult, but she had miles to go before getting out of the United States and into Germany at some point in this chase. She pulled out what maps she had to determine her best route in this damn state, the vehicle would not be a tremendous help now that she is in the public eye. She pulled out the newspaper, and smiled ear to ear with laughter, in her mind she was a hero, there must be readers that think she is great! She pores over the map and circles the two best routes through the woods, now she must estimate the miles and time it will take her to do so. With her current location and condition of her body, it could take her up to two weeks to cross the border. She will have many barriers such as the Forest Rangers, Game Wardens, or hunters she may have to avoid; her mind is broken with two shots of whiskey she passed out for the night. She wakes at 6 AM and sat by the river pondering her day, after pouring whiskey in her coffee she had her plan. Today was a day to set traps around her camp so anyone getting close would make noise, and quite possibly die. She ran barbed wire low to the ground around trees, grenades were wrapped in leaves with string attached, if the branch moved, the pin would drop and somebody would lose their head, and more. She scattered broken glass and set up rocks that would fall from a ledge and at least knock a person over, and she had a new toy, a flamethrower. After all that demanding work, she would walk as far as she could and record the time it took her, she could then evaluate her total time. As viscous as she was, her intelligence was not to be neglected. Susan was a genius with warfare, combat, engineering bombs, and she could hit a target with a pistol at one hundred yards, the norm is twenty-five yards. If a man saw her in a bar, she would be the one they would run to, beautiful dark eyes, and sexy as hell until you find out who she is! Exactly what Tolson thought back then and look at what had happened since he was with her, complete and utter chaos, and death. Susan sat up at her fire most of that night wondering where they all were. Tolson and his friends, police, and military, she kept killing them, did they give up? She will not let her guard down and trust that thought is factual. She had nightmares of her father being gunned down, the funny thing about people like her is that it is okay to murder someone, God help you if it is their family. The thought of killing Tolson and his friends kept her father's memories alive, the man was a nightmare, he trained his little girl to be who she is now and was eerily proud of that. Her childhood started out in a typical American family, toys, birthday parties, Christmases, and church, yes, the family went to church! She had friends, did well in school, played sports and sang in the choir, the neighbors never expected what an asshole their father really was. They had a wonderful house with a big yard and two vehicles, when most families had one, a facade that hid the demon inside him. He told people he worked for the government in a security role, but of course did not mention it was the German government. Sometimes at night she would think about the childhood days and gently fall asleep. There were no emotions attached to the dreams as most people had, just a period in their life. Her soul is dead inside her, she is nothing but a monster with breasts and a pretty smile! She aspired to go to college, but that would change under her father's rules, he had his own thoughts on her life, and it would be in the military. The Germans took care of him, but the day was coming to infiltrate more female spies into the organization, she was one of the first to be enlisted. With all these thoughts in her head, there is one thing her father took to his grave. The deal with the Germans was that if she did not join, he would have to execute her, the only thing he was not willing to do, so he played the hard ass soldier and parent. He never used the words, Love Respect, or even giving hugs, the German ice ran through his veins although he was American. It might be she has a hard exterior because of seeing her mother suffer through domestic violence, something she accepted as okay; thinking mom did something to deserve it, or at least her father would imply that. As this thought runs through her head she awakes and jumps to attention as she hears noise in her camp. Susan grabbed her military revolver and took cover behind her wall, as the noise increases, she is in awe of what she sees. A family of deer, beautiful creatures she admired so she would not harm them, she watched as the four of them snooped around and picked at what food was out. But the moment does not last, she must pack up and move, if there are deer, hunters are not far behind. As she is travelling northeast toward higher grounds a ring of rifle blasts goes off, no doubt they shot at the deer, she hears voices again and runs faster. There is a clearing ahead where she could change course but being out in the open for even one minute could put an end to her freedom permanently. Her option was to hide in a cave she had run by. It would only take her a few minutes to get there, the risk was going to have to take precedence over her flight. It was a small cave, so Susan was able to inconspicuously cover the opening with tree limbs and debris, nobody would notice it chasing wild animals for kill. She left an article of clothing on two of the paths heading out to the clearing on the hopes it distracts the hunters and sends them on their way, She could see three hunters arrive in her territory through her covered entryway, they stopped to pick up the clothes and talk over what might be going on. "Should we go to the south depot and report this to the rangers"? one of them said, this could be someone in a lot of trouble, few could survive these woods and the climate at night. After talking they decided to chase the trail, they were out there hunting so might as well check this out too. Susan stared at their warm hunting jackets and wondered how she could get one, she would have to distract one of them and pull them off the path into the woods. For once she was stumped, how do I go about this without the others gunning me down? she waited patiently to see if the men would split up for the search. As her luck would have it one of them took the path she had originally been on, she waited for them to get deeper to the dense part of the path and began digging herself out. She was certainly tough but in the mountains at night when the temperatures fall to below fifty degrees, a flannel shirt with a t-shirt no longer cuts it, even with a fire. She flanks the tree line and comes out ahead of the hunter, he is shocked when he sees her and stops in his tracks. She had her gun drawn and he ran right into it, his face now staring down the barrel of a German Lueger, a wrong move and he takes his last breath. Susan told him she just needed his jacket, which is all, but if he tried anything stupid including yelling out to his friends, his family would lose him and then she would go kill them as well. Shaking, he gently let his rifle fall to the ground amongst pine needles and remnants of fires and unzips his jacket. Susan reminds him that she knows they carry back up firearms, if he draws, she will kill him. He changes his mind because he cannot draw fast enough, and drops his sidearm as well, he handed her the jacket. So, what is next Susan? She was stunned. He said her name, "You are the lady on the run, correct? I am not looking for trouble with knowing what you are capable of, my friends and I are just out to hunt. She took a minute to decide on what to do, he would surely give the authorities the location and her description of his heavy, camouflage jacket. She turned as if to leave and spun around hitting him on the side of the head with her gun, he was down for the count, out cold and hopefully will not remember much when he wakes up, that is all she could do. Was her heart getting soft, why was he lucky enough to live? She had killed everybody that could identify her, but the gun would make too much noise, and his friends would come running, they knew the difference between a rifle shot and that of a handgun. She ran back to the cave, got her gear, and headed southwest, at least for three miles where she could rejoin the path to get to the northern part of the mountains. Doing this meant she would have to cover additional territory, a sacrifice that had to be made. Somewhere in her head a vision of Tolson and his boys chasing her through the hills made her quiver, they were tenacious and will not just forget about her. She had reached her safe place and dropped her gear, damn, it is only 8 AM and I am wiped out, the ground was soft and cold, but she had to rest. Susan could fight her way out of almost any situation, but she could not fight old age, she was forty-one years old now, one would never know looking at her. At 11 Am she awoke, surprised at the time she had a moment of panic and anxiety wondering where she had stopped and her next course of action. The water from the canteen was fresh from the pure mountain springs, something her body needed as she was at the onset of dehydration, a bad combination when you are cold. She cranked up a fire and sat close to it as she sipped coffee and water, she was hungry, but the smell of cooking would attract animals and people. She cut off a slab of the bread and lightly toasted it, for now this would suffice.

As Susan expected the hunters went into town to report this to the police, they dare not go to the rangers, she was too close and could kill them all. The more time they took, the further away from them she would be, was their thought process. After they told the officer in charge, he marched them over to Kane's office where the three amigos and Kane were diligently trying to figure out a proximity to where she was last seen. The officer was Sergeant Michael Hartmann of the Michigan State Police. His last name means "strong man" in English and that he was. Six foot, eight inches tall and three hundred pounds, he was a force to be reckoned with. Coincidently he is of German assent, but an American and one who protects the people and committed to the United States. He had been on the force for ten years and was Gray's partner at one time as a local policeman, he was saddened and distraught over his horrible death, and that of the others. The sergeant told the hunters to come back to the station when done here, he wanted to get more details from them, he could not sit there now when he had a town to watch over. The hunter who was assaulted was adamant about not return to that area of the woods but would draw out on the map the exact location, "she threatened to kill me and my family, I am not risking that." All the information was still posted through Kane's office, the man went to the first map and circled the area, which is her location about two miles from Cranston Ridge pass through. It was named after Jeremiah L. Cranston, a pioneer in the early 1900s, he was a great scout and guide and feared nothing. The right man to trudge through the mountains creating travel ways for the future. He was cutting wood on a wintry day in January of 1916 and slipped off the side of the mountain, tragically dying. His cabin has been maintained by town folks over the years and used as a hunting cabin or rented out to families on camping trips. The men now had a starting point and if they got their late in the day, they would have shelter where they could build a fire as well. Tolson questioned the men on the best route to the area from town, Mountain Pass road one of them replied, know where it is? Yes, we do, that is the road we were tracking Susan when the explosion came from Mary's house, they all got quiet for a moment, the hunters had nothing to add, they had known her since their school days. After they depart, the men talk openly about going after Susan, weighing out the risks versus rewards, Tolson did not mind leading the way, he had nobody waiting for him at home when he eventually gets there. The decision is made to head to the road at 8 PM, it will be dark enough to scout around, "dark clothes and dark face paint are required gentlemen, we will get plenty of rest, stay out of sight all day" ordered Tolson. Kane walked to their hotel at 5:30 PM to treat them to dinner, he had all his gear with him, "where do you think you're going," with you he replied. The three did not like the idea, you have a business to run, with you gone it will only raise more suspicion and concern for the town. "No offense said Riley, but the last thing we need is a bunch of backwoods yahoos chasing down a proven murderer." Kane agreed with them and stated he would be their contact in town, they all had police radios and could now conduct their mission. They left promptly at 8 PM driving through town without lights on and gave Kane a signal they were out of town. As the approach their destination they cannot help but think if she is lurking in the dark, waiting to kill them all, but they are soldiers in their blood and not cowards. Even though Tolson made a mistake by leaving his unit to screw Susan, he had nerves and guts like steel, he never backed down from fighting to save friends and allies. The plan was to stay together until they set up camp, one mile up the hill there is a spot that drops down behind the cave Susan was in, they will operate from that site. Riley radioed Kane softly and told him they are in place. He replied that he will track time, if he has not heard from them by 11 PM, he is getting in his car, so they had better call him if they want to keep him safe. Once camp is set up, they review the location the hunter gave them and decide to split the area three ways, keep your radios and firearms ready, call out for help if you see here said Tolson, he took the lead as their commander. The men break out and there is silence for the first two hours except for the animals, Tolson performs a radio check, all clear on their end. As Whiteway heads northeast he is struck by the most excruciating pain in his right leg, the barbed wire traps Susan set, have been exposed, he calls out and warns the others to use more caution and he is heading back to camp; Riley and Tolson head back to tend to him medically. When the three return they notice Whiteway's leg is shredded and requires stitches, he is limping to keep weight off it, the more weight, the more blood loss. Tolson radios

Kane for help and reports the incident, "we cleaned the wound and put a tourniquet on it, but he needs a doctor, Kane says "on my way with the doctor, we do not want you seen going into his office." Kane scoops up Dr. Reynolds, a true professional and highly rated doctor in the area for twenty years, he brought his bag full of antiseptics, nova cane to numb it, sutures, and gauze to protect it from infection. When they arrived, there is no sign of anyone, the men hid deeper in the woods. When Kane radioed for them, Riley said he will meet them at the road, there are booby traps everywhere. He led Kane and the doctor safely to their camp and went back to hide their vehicle, "you two will be staying overnight with us" he said, but you are not leaving the camp, or I will shoot you myself. After fifteen minutes of pulling any barbed wire strands out of his leg by the fire, he cleaned it and then stuck him with a needle of nova cane and a belt of whiskey, the perfect combination for surgery in the woods. The good doctor had Tolson shine his light on the leg, he was not going to stitch it up if there was dirt or debris in there, the bacteria would be sewed inside, and he would lose his leg all together! After twenty minutes, the leg was sewn, he had to put stitches deep inside as the gash was close to arteries and had to be secured with more sutures. He gently wrapped the leg and advised the other two to make a crutch for him out of tree limbs, they will wrap it in a jersey so he does not puncture his arm pit; that is one thing he could not bring with him, people would have notice crutches being tossed into the car. The doctor gave them medication to reduce the swelling, and to help him sleep, the longer he was off the leg, the better his odds of infection are reduced. Dr. Reynolds stayed near him all night constantly checking the bandages for blood, it was minimal and expected due to the nature of the injury. Whiteway passed out on a sleeping bag which made them all happy, he needed rest, we would not be able to push him too hard. The men shared conversation and whiskey trying to figure out the next move. Kane volunteered again, but this time to take Whiteway's place, he will slow them down and be a crippled target for Susan. Tolson and Riley walked away from the camp to discuss, the answer is still no Mr. Kane, we are sorry, but you cannot disappear from town. It will draw too much attention, and people will figure out where you are, furthermore, you could put us all at a higher risk by doing so. Kane reluctantly agreed knowing they are right; he and the doctor will leave at 5 AM tomorrow to be in town without getting noticed by anyone. But what of Whiteway, will he stay or go to town with them? A tough decision but if he is spotted with a wound that is bandaged up and walking with a crutch, their office would be flooded with people wanting answers, they have been through this before. As the men talk Dr. Reynold suggested he and Kane give Hartmann an update of where they are and inform them of the injury, they agreed that is best. The next morning Hartmann receives a call at 5:30 AM on his house phone, when he hears the voice, he jumps ahead and says I'll be right there. His wife is a sound sleeper, he kisses her forehead and leaves her a note that he had to get into town early. They had been married for seven years with no children, she was not able to conceive, they thought it was fun trying, who knows, someday a miracle would bless their marriage and home. He arrives at Kane's office and he along with the doctor tell the entire story. Hartmann himself is overly concerned about the men in the hills, especially with one being injured. He deems it best to leave them alone for the day as Kane assured him, they are not tracking today, it is time to rest. The officer expects communication as to the men's activities, he finds it hard to believe that Tolson and Riley would not build cover for Whiteway and hit the road in search of Susan. He wants an update every two hours and if help is needed, he will send the State Police up the mountain, for now, he will let them do what they feel must be done. Not that he condones violence or murder, he understands the whole situation, but he still must follow the law; he will give them little leeway with this. He warned them against any executions, they would get at least fifteen years for the crime, and he had no problem being the arresting officer. The sun was strong over the top of the trees and temperatures reached eighty, even in the mountains, their young Private was heating up. They had secured the area and found Susan's old hiding spot in the cave, he would be safe there once they covered the entrance, they carried him to the lake and helped him wash up, feeling cooler and should now be able to sleep. Tolson filled two canteens for him, and Riley made up a bed for comfort, the last thing he needed was a campfire, they checked his radio and off the two went. Their plan was to head northeast and take the path where the hunters found her clothing, the trees provided cover from the sun and hopefully Susan.

CHAPTER 13

They scoured the hills for three hours but knew they had to get back to check on their fallen friend, they took a path south of their original pass, Whiteway's safety is most important to them. As they approach camp Tolson calls over the radio into Kane for his update, they report zero sightings and no signs of a camp she may have built. Kane went to answer when a woman's familiar voice interrupts, "hey assholes, it is the person you fear most, Susan, you can all go to hell." "Your friend is chicken shit, he whimpered like a maimed cat when I found him, stupid putting him in the cave I used for shelter, do not worry he is not dead, YET"! She held the mike button down and laughed in a man-like roar while stepping on Whiteway's leg, he screamed in pain and agony but found time to yell out their location. She took her knee and knocked his head in with it, he was semi unconscious now, dizzy, and blurry vision came quickly. She had one more thing to say to the small radio group, "the ad in the paper states I killed three hundred and seventy-nine soldiers, you never factored in the Battle of Vimy Ridge." I dropped another one hundred and seventy-one Americans because it was fun. I really enjoyed it, that gives me an even five hundred dead, so realize you are not smart enough or fast enough to capture me before I leave the country." Hartmann drove to Kane's office, "how can we get them to change channels without her knowing"? he sent out a morse code message using beeps on the radio for the channel, Susan could break codes, but this was in Russian, something she was not familiar with or fluent in. The team switched their channels and had a twenty-second communication, no time for Susan to figure it out and track them. The message meant Hartmann and the others were on the way up to help, but he had not reached out to his peers yet. The noise of the tires and engines from several police cars would surely send her scampering with her hostage, whether he could run or not. It took the men just fifteen minutes to gather and get to the Mountain road cut off in search of the men, they too must be stealth like during their movement. The three townies got out of the car and started their trek to the camp Tolson and Riley built, they were able to jog at a fast pace and get there within twelve minutes. Hartmann walks up to them both and slugs them each in the face "you idiots, Susan is right, what were you thinking leaving him in that cave, now we have a hostage situation asshole." Kane yelled out, "We have bigger problems sergeant, fighting amongst ourselves will not fix them." Hartmann apologized; he knew Kane was right. They both spoke up and said he was right, if Whiteway dies, it is our fault, we need to forget this and make our next move. The party agreed to split up and get moving, Kane and Hartmann would check the cave for clues, evidence, footprints, anything to get a bead on Whiteway. Tolson looked at Riley and said, "time to really man up my friend, we need to go separate ways but stay in touch with everyone." A handshake and a brief manly hug sent them out into the wilderness with the hopes of finding their dear friend, at this moment they could care less about Susan. Whiteway was a sharp guy, he began leaving blood trails without Susan knowing, she was busy reading maps and getting her bearings. As much pain as he was experiencing due to her kicking his injury, she inadvertently did him a favor. "I hope you die a slow, painful death you pile of garbage" he thought to himself, he did not want to rile her by saying it aloud and change her focus toward him and his attempts to lead the rescue party her way. He also cut off a piece of his pants and shirt and tied them to a stick hanging of different trees, if the police brought dogs out tomorrow, they would find him. Susan was not aware of an additional sidearm he concealed in his left sock, strapped to his calf, it was his right leg that had got injured, and she focused only on that one, a big mistake for such a great spy! He was weak and being dragged around the woods on oversized roots which hurt his back and head. He thought he could shoot her, but his vision sucked, and his nervous system was damage to where he shook too much, leaving the gun as a clue would be more beneficial. Susan felt she had a good path to take so she ordered him off the ground to walk as best he could, he had a crutch that she would beat him with if he did not use it to walk. Whiteway was not one to complain especially to a cold-blooded killer, but he spouted out that he needs rest, he cannot do this all night, "If you are going to kill me, do it now bitch." Susan looked at him with a huge smile and said, "you may just have more balls than your friends, sit down soldier we shall camp here, but one signal to your posse and I will end your life." Besides, she wanted to torment him and piss off Tolson, Riley, and the others chasing her. If they felt he was always in jeopardy in her presence, they would move slowly and not risk further harm, and she was right. The men had slowed down but were still on the move in and out of paths and trees making sure to check in, Tolson and Riley were about two miles apart, the others were further south and four miles from them. Hartmann sends a code to the two "mountain men" he nicknamed them for simplicity after nearly knocking their teeth out, he thought humor could band them together, it worked. Kane came across some of Whiteway's things in the cave and he scored a bonus, Susan must have dropped some things out of her duffle bag, her German Ruger pistol, and a blonde wig, she was now dark hair and did not have an option of walking into a store for a new one. She would more than likely find out later when she goes to swap them out to turn to lighter hair, this is the first time any of the men felt that had a hold on Susan. It was not as good as having her ties to a stake and lighting it on fire, but it was damn good enough to keep their spirits high! "Great work Kane, Tolson spoke up, great work and thank you for caring about our friend, he is a good soldier and even better man"! The two make their way to the cave to meet up and collect their thoughts, they lit a fire and heated up some food, nothing great, just beans, ham, and some rolls. They toasted some shots to those who died and to their success in getting Whiteway alive, the two soldiers shared stories of their young friend. Tolson asked Hartmann if he was married, and did they have children? "I am married to a great woman, but right now we cannot have children, we will see how the future goes." Tolson stated the reason he asked is because the young, injured man with a crazed woman in the woods has a wife and a seven-month-old baby at home, we want to make sure he gets back there to Colorado safely. He has not been in contact with er for over four months for her safety. Hartmann told them he will call in State Troopers tomorrow and have them rescue, Kane suggested get a helicopter and search the area from the sky, something they all neglected due to the taste of blood in their mouths for the woman responsible for five hundred war assassinations, and more here in the Midwest and Northeast regions. Tolson loved the idea, scare her by letting her know we have better visibility, and do not storm the mountains with one hundred police officers, the pressure needs to get to Susan, it will take more than a helicopter, but it is a good start. State policeman and helicopter pilot Tyler Sykes heard about this and volunteered his time on his day off, he was fully armed, and the chopper was equipped with tear gas and two shotguns. Hartmann gave him the coordinates and asked him to be there at 8 AM, he showed up at 6:30 wanting her to make a move that would push her into the open. He waved down at the men as he flew overhead, they gave him the peace sign with two fingers and saluted as he went by. The radio was silenced when they abruptly heard "chopper Z33476 to commander, come in please, commander, are you there". "Copy, it is Hartmann here, go ahead." The pilot reported he was by the waterfall at Grove Canyon, there is a man's body on the ground, and I have eyes on Susan, she is heading directly north through the pass after the canyon. The men clasped their hands as if they were saying prayers, "what is she wearing" replied Tolson, hang tight sir was the pilot's response. He She has a green army style jacket on, khaki-colored pants, work boots and dark hair. I will stay on my path, but you better check out your friend on the ground. There is a clearing where the chopper can land, let me know when you are near the area, and I will land and get you all out. They were under one mile from the canyon, but the chopper had no place to land to pick them up, it would take them fifteen minutes by foot, in the meantime the pilot stalked Susan from the air. He followed her over the trees, it did not look like she had a plan, she seemed lost and kept turning her head toward the sky to see where he was. The pilot heard a call out from the guys, Whiteway was alive, he played possum and made her think he must have died from the wound and heat stroke, when she heard the chopper, she ran to the woods without checking his pulse. When the chopper landed the men rushed Whiteway to it and laid him on the floor, for his safety and theirs, the chopper pilot took off immediately headed to the hospital. It took only ten minutes in the chopper to reach their destination, Whiteway was rushed into surgery to repair the open wound, the men would stay there until they knew he was safe and going to live. Dr. Reynolds happened to be on duty, and he rushed to the emergency operating room to repair his leg again, Whiteway was thrilled to see him. After surgery they sent him to a private recovery room, Hartmann placed plain clothes detectives throughout the hospital floors to provide security. The doctor came out and let them know he was going to be fine. Fortunately, the infection did not expedite through his body, and I was able to save the leg, with rest he will be ready to leave in four days. Tolson made his way to the nurses' station and asked politely to use the phone, he had to advise Whiteway's wife of the situation. He dialed the number, she picked up the phone and Tolson said, "hi Melissa this is Private Tolson, I have news for you, your husband is going to be okay, he is in the hospital right now, but I cannot tell you where he is." He backtracked and gave her a very brief synopsis of what had happened and said he had to hang up. She begged him to have Thomas call her later, he would do his best. The men only cared about him right now wherever "Crazy Susan" was, they were confident she was locked down in their area and no way to break through the barrier of law enforcement agents. Hartmann and the pilot were heading back to the search area, the two friends must stay behind for added security, Tolson reminded them to please remember what she is capable of, do not assume anything, her head is wired all wrong. The sergeant said their radio would be on an open channel, her path is clear, and we should be able to have her in sight within the hour. Tolson and Riley advised the officer on guard they were going for coffee, do not let anyone near or in his room please, we will only be five minutes. They were relieved upon arriving back at the ward that the officer was there and not even a nurse had entered the room, he wanted to go home for dinner, so they excused him, he promised to be back for his 8PM-3AM watch. As he walked away, he turned and said to the men "we all care about your friend and this whole mess, all the officers are on your side, just know that." The men thanked him and smiled, their turn to guard the room.

CHAPTER 14

Riley took the hallway, door accesses, and doctor and nurses' lounge. Tolson covered elevators, nurses' station, and bathrooms. Police were strategically placed on the two floors above and below Whiteway's room, they also had the parking area and cafeteria covered. There was an office in uniform at the door continuously, he was always guarded during recovery. Hartmann had landed in the clearing with Pilot Sykes and immediately saw smoke, a campfire that had recently been extinguished, our girl cannot be too far, he said to the sergeant. The two men grabbed the weapons out of the chopper and headed to the site of the smoldering wood, they flanked the camp she made so they did not walk straight into a trap. Hartmann told Sykes what to look for as far as traps, they circled the area and the opening to the trails. They carried sticks to poke around but also needed to remember about grenades and potential land mines that would splatter them into one thousand pieces. In a burst Hartmann caught

Susan out of the corner of his eye, "there she goes, after her, let's move, watch for gunfire, and shoot to kill." As she ran around a tree Sykes lined her up in his scope of his Winchester hunting rifle and blasted a tear through her jacket into her abdomen, "I hit her boss, she is down." Do not rush after her she is armed, we cannot trust her actions, I will call Tolson and get them out here." He picked up his radio and frantically shouted for Tolson and Riley, "get out here, get out here, Sykes shot her she is down, fifteen minutes east of the canyon near the old ranger station," "on our way hold your positions and stay low" barked Tolson. He yelled down the hallway where Riley was, he was already running toward him as he had his radio as well, the adrenaline was pumping and heart rates increased, they needed this, hopefully Susan was hit well enough to keep her done for the arrest. As they speed to support the men, they nearly avoid a head on collision, they are sweating and tasting bloody revenge more than ever, this douchebag cannot get away again, we must stop her now. When the get to the meeting spot the men are not anywhere to be found, their hearts sink and stomachs have a knot in them, both their thoughts went right to murder, son of a bitch, she got them. As they approach the path they hear noise behind them, both men turn with guns pointed its Hartmann and Sykes, "you morons, we could have killed you, where is the whore?" snapped Riley, it was his turn to pop Hartmann in the mouth and he did it with force knocking him backwards to the ground, Sykes was a cop but just the pilot today. At that moment gunfire opened, and bullets were tearing through the woods toward the cave and the men, Susan was ranting angrily threatening that this will be their last day on earth, she has gone overboard and is like a crazed, rabid, wild animal now. They quickly jump to cover until they can pinpoint her location in hopes they can put an end to this crap, none of them has a clear shot and if they stick their heads out, someone will surely die here today. Sykes is the one who heard her gun jamming but she had more, they sit back for a moment and wait, is she still there? The desire to charge into the woods and grab her was enticing to them all, but they would rather go home in the chopper not a body bag. From the clearing the men see hunters up on the far ridge with dogs, Riley was the quickest, the rest covered him with gunfire while he muscled his way up the hiking path to get to them. He arrived in record time, just six minutes up the steep hill and over the ridge, as soon as he got there, he ordered the men to get down, they dropped to their bellies and covered their dogs. Riley explained the situation, they already knew it had to be Susan in the papers and the talk around town for weeks is she is still in the area, the hunters asked what they could do. Riley started by telling them they could use the dogs to grab her scent but warned them they could be shot and might die; she does not care about life. The hunters were worried, but they would allow their dogs to get closer to pick up her scent, but not close where she could shoot them, Riley agreed, he loved dogs. There were four men total, he positioned two on the ridge and pointed to her estimated location, the other two went down with him to meet the guys. The hunters knew the police officers well, one of them played football with Hartmann and the other dated his sister for two years. Tolson would lead everyone in, he would take the first bullet like a good military leader would do for anyone. Riley left a radio with the hunters on the ridge. The last thing they need is to get sniped from up top, they had their assignment, if they get a call to come down, they will charge from the rear of what used to be her camp. Susan was hurting and she knew it, admitting it to herself was more painful than the wound, which was twice she had been shot by this group chasing her. A calmness came over her, she had to remain levelheaded if she were to get out of this. She could not pick up their conversations anymore, she had dropped her radio running into the woods. Her first mission, shelter to get a look at the wound, she had limited medical supplies left after the last bullet she took. Heading northeast again she took a new pass to an old, abandoned shack, but would she be safe there? The guys would see it as easily as she did, encroach and attack, she would not get out alive and that was not in her plan. She opted to keep moving up the mountain and find a hiding place, her abdomen was bleeding and with each step spurted out more, she looked to the west and saw an opening in an old mine shaft of a sort. As she approached it, she noticed it was already covered with debris and if she could find an entry point, she would be okay for a few hours. Susan found a way in through thick brush; she emptied out the few things she had remaining out of the duffle bag and walked out of the mine. She knew the men were smart and they are not giving up, so she tossed the duffle bag and scattered clothes in the woods heading northeast, the dogs would certainly help her by pulling in that direction; the mine was not far, her feet carried her as quickly as they could, and she hid back inside her new lair. Inside she had no choice but to light a small fire to see her wound, it was not pretty. The slug was deep inside, and she was afraid to pull the bullet out and risk further infection, but she heated up her knife and began the process. It hurt like hell, she had no whiskey left to try to ease the pain, it had to be used to clean the wound after. She put a stick in her mouth like a dog and chomped down, she could not scream as it may bring attention. As it dug in deeper, she teared up in pain but toughed it out, the slug was removed after ten minutes, she had to be careful not to hit vital organs. After pouring a few drops of whiskey into it she patted it with gauze and began to stitch it closed. Afterward she felt weak, doused the fire, and passed out from the blood less and stress of her less than stellar surgery, but she was not after pretty, just keep the blood in. If the men neared the mine entry, she would hear sticks breaking and rocks falling, they were bigger than her and could not shimmy in quietly. The men would be out all night searching not knowing she is west of their location, so far, her plan was working.

CHAPTER 15

The next morning Hartmann sensed something was wrong, "guys, we travelled miles overnight and I am convinced she did not head northeast, what do you think Tolson?" Tolson stated his agreement with the sergeant and made mention how the dogs stopped sniffing and chasing. Hunting dogs usually do not give up on their prey, once again they were faced with agreeing on a course of action, this bitch is killing us Riley laughed, then apologized realizing that is her goal. The men would head back west and when they reached their original starting point by the cave they would split two paths, each group taking a hunter and a dog. Tolson wanted to peek inside the cave and make sure she was not there, with the long barrel of his rifle sticking in ahead of him, Riley shined his flashlight, once it was cleared, they went in to check for anything she may have left behind. Kane first heard the radio crackle with someone trying to connect, he spoke into it knowing it was Dr. Reynolds at the hospital, he had the only other radio they were using. A clear signal finally came through. "I thought you boys would like to know that Thomas Whiteway was put on a train with two undercover FBI agents, he is on his way home to Colorado, his wife has been alerted." The men sighed with a huge relief, their friend was safe and out of danger, they vowed to call him the minute they take Susan in, she was cornered in those woods somewhere and in trouble physically. They split up and continued southwest, Susan would not want to reach higher elevations, her lungs would get less oxygen and therefore push her heart to work harder. In her current condition she had a considerable risk of dying, she would rather be killed by the search party and die with honor, Germany would be proud as would her dead father. Kane is the first one to call out on the radio, "guys, get your asses over to the abandoned cabin about a half mile from your location, head east, we found clues, copy." That's a big copy Tolson replied, "We are on our way sir." Kane loved the respect of being called "sir," he was older and felt that is the way people should be treated. When they got to the cabin and opened the door, there was Kane and his hunter, each of them holding a prize. Susan's canteen and her maps were left there, this was great news, she was finding her way around blinded. As excelled as she was in combat and survival, they knew her situation was bad and no matter what she is no longer who she was at the start of the chase weeks ago. An advantage for them as she would not be thinking clearly nor active enough to fight them, but she still had a gun and hunting knife to defend herself. Hartmann suggested when they go back out start yelling "Susan we are coming for you, we know you are injured badly, give it up." It could rope her into responding and they would get a better gauge of her location. What they did not know is she was deep inside a mine shaft, even if she did hear them, she was certainly not coming out into the open. The men conducted their mission, yelling from every angle of the woods while looking for footprints or drag marks, those would come from Susan trawling brush along to erase her steps leading to her hideouts she had made. She awoke at 8:30 AM and had no bearings of where she was, her lightheaded mind and sickness from the wound had crushed her energy and spirit; with no penicillin to take she had to tough it out. Vertigo kept her from standing too long for fear she would fall over and hit her head on rock, vomit erupted as soon as she sat back down, she had never felt so sick. With no food and minimal water in her spare canteen, she had to figure out where to get some, there is no way she can make it down the mountain to a farm or a house to steal these items. She was pissed at herself for not bringing her silencer, she could easily kill an animal and cook it. Susan remembered the lake, she could go catch fish, the protein would help with her strength and then rub fish oil on her wound. Since the angry mob was hunting her down, she will have to wait until dark or early morning the next day, fish bite much better in the morning. The men set up a new camp three miles from the mine and made lunch, they had not eaten since the last night and were slowing down. Knowing Susan's odds of running like a gazelle through the woods were zero to none, they were chill and decided to take a long break themselves. Tolson set up a guard schedule "we need at least four hours sleep each, you guys get shuteye, I'll take first post." At 2:30 in the afternoon the mountain skies opened and began dumping pouring rain on the men and their camp, they scurried to grab their belongings and take cover under trees. Once out of the rain they built a lean to shelter with a thatched roof to keep them dry, it was good enough for a rush job. Susan awoke to the storm, it was pounding down on the old wooden planks and the brush she used for cover, now was the best opportunity for her to fish. She crawled quietly to the opening being careful not to stand or poke her head out just yet. The estimation to the lake was ten minutes but she was cold and damp, the atmosphere outside the mine was raw, a risky trip at best. Her intelligence had not faded as badly as her body, she took some branches with lots of leaves on them and used them as a shield. They were draped over her back like a raincoat would be, if anyone came around, she could crouch, and they would be none the wiser; brilliant. She had no time to be concerned with them right now, she was starving and would pass out if she did not eat, it would be days before she could even move at half speed. She was fortunate enough to catch two large bass, great for cooking on an open fire, she would scale and gut them with her knife. Once the fire was built and the fish clean, she shoved a long stick through their bodies and put them on a homemade rotisserie. At four pounds each, she would eat now and warm up the rest later for dinner, she had no idea of how long she would be holed up there. The rain never subsided until early the next morning at 4 AM, when they men got up, they put their things out in the sun to dry them which took two hours. Susan did not have that option, it would leave her site vulnerable, she chose to go outside for an hour to dry off and warm up. She wondered if this were her "last hurrah" the men have worn her down and she was pigeonholed in the mine, she would not live much longer in there without the essentials of life. Tired and angry that they found her general location, she had to plan her escape regardless of the result, she had enough of this shit. Her plan was to wait until dark again, look for fire or smoke from their camp, they had moved closer to her without knowing; but her instincts told her they were near. Hartmann, Kane, Riley, and Tolson were also done with this mess, "this shit ends today, I want her captured or dead by 5PM tonight men" instructed Tolson. Hartmann spoke up and said, "I am an officer of the law, I cannot allow you to take her down in cold blood, if you are not in eminent danger, we have to bring her in." The trust they had built as a team led to respect, they agreed to do their best to respect his authority. Hartmann was not fooled, he knew in his mind Riley and Tolson were out for revenge, no matter what he had to say. Susan had decided to make a move, she could head east on a straight terrain and use the hills to slide down, this would take a load of pressure off her body. Her childhood came back to her, and she thought about winter in New Jersey when all her friends would go sledding in the winter snow. The leafy tree branched would serve as her toboggan to protect her body, she had to figure the right time to go, she leaned against a wall to ponder her judgement of the men's locations. Did it really matter? They were sure to get her within this area, she was just going to have to pick a time and go, not backing out. Kane went to take a leak when he noticed some footsteps in the muddy ground, he finished and ran back to the camp. Once he told them they picked up their weapons and rushed to the scene, they all grinned with a sense of success. Hartmann surveyed the area and as he scanned the area saw a sign, "half a mile to Greystone Mine," shit guys, she is there, no doubt. Kane and Hartmann felt foolish as they grew up there but overlooked the memory of its once thriving business. It was dangerous and many men died working it, the owners paid the families and closed it for good in 1913. one of the first mines to close in that region. They closed in on the mine's entrance and Hartmann turned the corner, a shot rang out and he was hit in the chest and knocked back, fortunately the bullet missed the organs. He was fine but he was unconscious after hitting the ground. Kane immediately called Dr. Reynolds and advised him of the situation," do not move him, I am on my way" Thanks doc, please hurry. The men surrounded the front and sides, knowing she would claw and fight her way out to the best of her abilities, this will not be a happy ending for her. Tolson took the back, there were broken boards, and no doubt Susan would try to escape there. Doc arrived and tended to Hartmann was dizzy and could not think straight, Dr. Reynolds gave hm some pain relief and propped his head up slightly on a sleeping pad and gave him instructions to stay still. He will watch over him while the others take care of their business, he reached into the sergeant's coat and pulled his long barrel .38 caliber pistol out of its holster. The doctor could fire a weapon so he felt he could defend them both if need be. Susan reared her ugly head out back and Tolson saw her, before she could act, his revolver was stuck in her right temple, a sure kill. "Hey lover boy, long time no see" she stated, he slapped her in the face as hard as he could and she hit the ground, her gun went flying into the trees. With blood dribbling out of her mouth, Tolson looked to the sky and asked his mom and God to forgive him for hitting a woman; not that she qualified as one by any means. She began spouting off about the murders, trying to rile him, but he would not bite, there was no sense in giving her a lecture, she had no heart. He made sure none of the others were around, they were on high alert at their posts, and he knew Hartmann was down. He bowed his head down at her with a look of hatred and evil, mirroring her attitude and thoughts. Tolson opened his mouth and said, "you silenced our five hundred, time for you to be quiet," he raised his pistol and put two bullets in her head, killing her instantly; the others thought the worst as they ran to him. They were relieved to see him standing in good health, the men embraced and broke down to tears, what a long, horrific ordeal. All those innocent people who died here in the states, moms, ex-soldiers, woman and children, police officers, a brutal butchering they wish never happened, but it is finally over. They headed back to town after throwing her body into the car, Riley wanted to toss her off the cliff, but they had to bring her to town for a burial, the citizens would want to see proof she was no longer a threat. A kid riding his bicycle saw the two cars riding into town, one with Dr. Reynolds and the injured Hartmann riding shotgun, and the deceased female devil in the back. The second car carrying Kane, Tolson, and Riley, all smiling with relief, not humor. They felt like they were back in the war, dirty, smelly, tattered clothing, and hungry. The child fled ahead yelling as he drove through town to come out and look, "they got her, they got her."

People cheered as if at a football game, the men were heroes, they sacrificed everything going after her and lost loved ones along the way. They helped Hartmann out of the car, he was bleeding and bruised and barely awake, they did not know if he was dying, they loved this man as much as they loved Mary. There was one thing left for the men to do, call Private Thomas Whiteway, and give him the news. He was elated of course, and his health had improved drastically, he invited them all out to Colorado to spend time on his father's farm and ranch. "As soon as Hartmann is better, we will call you, all our best friend!" As Hartmann was being placed in a wheelchair he called Tolson over in privacy. "Look, I know what you did, even though I was out cold, I am not a stupid man." You have no injuries, scars, or bruises, I need to know one thing; did you enjoy it"? "Hell, yes I did sir but will never admit it outside this conversation." Hartmann told him to lean down and gave him a huge hug and whispered in his ear, "I am proud of your leadership and actions as a soldier, great job"! I will not repeat that either said Hartmann, with a smile both men part ways.